MESSAGE
FROM THE VILLAGE

The Epoch B Foundation, New York.

MESSAGE FROM THE VILLAGE

by Perdita Huston

Copyright © 1978 by Perdita Huston
Published by The Epoch B Foundation
P.O. Box 1972, Grand Central Station,
New York, New York 10017.

Library of Congress Cataloging in Publication Data

Huston, Perdita, 1936-
  Message from the village.

  1. Underdeveloped areas—Family size. 2. Under-developed areas—Birth
control. 3. Rural women—Interviews. 4. Underdeveloped areas—Social
conditions.
  I. Title.
HQ760.H87   301.41′2′091724   78-6045

ISBN: 931730-01-5

For those whose words
are the basis of this book,
with admiration and respect.

CONTENTS

ACKNOWLEDGEMENTS

A word of thanks to Mrs Helvi Sipila, who led the United Nations activities for the International Women's Year, 1975. This book is a modest contribution to the effort that began in 1975 to clarify and strengthen the role of women in the development process.

It goes without saying that this book would not have been possible had it not been for the patience and caring of countless women and men who were willing to counsel and guide me throughout my travels. They served as interpreters and as wise counselors. Although I cannot mention each by name, I am greatly indebted to them.

I am indebted also to the United Nations Fund for Population Activities, the agency which sponsored this book, and, especially, to Tarzie Vittachi, who originally encouraged me to undertake the project, and to his colleague, Jyoti Singh, who helped me to overcome obstacles at every stage. Also of UNFPA, Sabina Wenzel was consistently helpful and understanding as was Dr Dipak Bhatia, Regional Coordinator in Cairo.

Amy Koide (San Diego) was a conscientious and friendly help-mate throughout the production of the manuscript, as were Hortense Boutell, Evelyn Harrison and Sandra Nichols who were willing to read it and make suggestions for its improvement. I am particularly grateful to Lois O'Neill whose fine editing and encouragement helped me enormously.

Several individuals encountered during the months of travel showed more than professional concern for my mission and were particularly helpful in its completion. They are: Cherifa Mehrez (Egypt), Lily Bett (Kenya), Mrs. N.S.C. Perera and Marina Fernando (Sri Lanka), Lucia Mier Y Teran de Munoz and Wilma Vilunya Diskin (Mexico).

Lastly, I am particularly grateful to my mother, Marion Brooks Huston, and to Harry Harding whose help and encouragement over the years enabled me to undertake this project.

Perdita Huston
La Jolla

INTRODUCTION

One of the sad—and even dangerous—things about "development" work is that those whose task is to think and make plans to improve the lives of the world's villagers too often lose touch with the feeling and thinking of the villages. Many development programmes thereby become insensitive, unresponsive and therefore irrelevant and flounder expensively because they fail to excite the active involvement of the very people they are designed to benefit. How many planners and "developmentalists" who speak with great facility and sentimentality about "the grass roots" have seen one lately? This creeping remoteness draws a sort of strength and authority from the silence of the village which is taken as acquiescence. And, what is more, since literacy and wisdom are often regarded as being synonymous that silence fortifies the notion that the people of the village are not able to judge for themselves what their needs are. A great deal of effort is therefore spent on designing strategies for getting "the message" from the urban centre to the grass roots. This process cannot continue with impunity for long as the villagers of Barelli showed in their massive rejection of that kind of attitude at the last general election in India. It is time that more than lip service is paid to the dictum that communicating messages is a two-way undertaking.

This is why the United Nations Fund for Population Activities has assisted the Epoch B Foundation, the publisher of this book, and Perdita Huston, the author, to begin the task of bringing the message *from* the village on the feelings, attitudes and needs on population and development as expressed by a sampling of women in 130 villages spread over three continents. Their views and the views of the author do not necessarily represent those of the UNFPA or any of its officials. However, many of these views challenge some of the familiar assumptions made by administrators, planners and workers in the population field and all of them are worth taking seriously although Mrs. Huston lays no claim to have brought back all the messages from her sisters in the Third World.

Tarzie Vittachi
Chief, Information and Public Affairs Division
United Nations Fund for Population Activities

"I am nothing; I am a beast. Look at me.
No, I don't want my children to be beasts like me . . ."

A woman of the less-developed world

FOREWORD

*"If we are patient enough to give time for
ideas to emerge from the grassroots,
maybe we can strike the balance."*
Phoebe Asieyo[1], Nairobi, 1976

To trace my interest in the population question—or why I
wanted to record the conversations that comprise this report—I
would have to return to a small village of a less developed nation
where I worked in the early 1960s. The only literate woman
among a population of 15,000, I was in title a social worker, but I
served also as nurse, letter-writer, marriage counselor, food
distributor, and midwife.

As I lived and worked with those villagers I learned to
respect their wisdom and their constant struggle to improve
their lives. I was particularly touched by the lives of the peasant
women who searched ceaselessly for food, firewood, dung,
water, and hope.

During that period, several of those women dared ask me,
"What is it you do NOT to have a child each year?" They sought
to learn how to control the number and spacing of their children
but contraceptive methods were prohibited in their country. On
several occasions, I witnessed the results of a woman's attempt
to avoid having a new mouth to feed. Their desperation shook
me.

It was then that I, like so many others, came to believe that
the availability of contraceptive methods would be welcomed
by women. It would permit them to partake of life more fully, by
freeing them from the continuous child-bearing that they sought
to limit.

But family-planning programs introduced since that time
have been only sporadically successful. We continue to wonder

[1]Director, Welfare Association of Kenya.

why some thrive while others flounder? Official statistical reports provide few answers. We continue to guess, to send investigative teams, to spend more funds. Progress remains slow.

It seemed to me that some answers might come from the proposed "clients" of family-planning efforts: the poor, uneducated women of the world's developing regions. With this in mind, during 1976 and 1977 I traveled to remote villages to talk with rural women, hoping to learn from them how they saw their lives, what changes were taking place around them, and what they sought for their children. I hoped to document attitudes that might help clarify what is needed in family-planning programs. My thought was to reverse the habitual one-way process of communications—from planners to villagers.

The countries I visited—Kenya, Sudan, Egypt, Sri Lanka, Mexico, and Tunisia—were chosen for their cultural differences and because each had maintained a family-planning program for several years. No formal questionnaire was used; these were not research interviews. We were women talking together, about our families, our children, our lives. I told them about my mother; they told me about theirs.

"But," I have been asked, "how can you be sure they weren't just telling you what they thought you wanted to hear?"

This is a valid question. In reply, I can only describe the process of inquiry. Upon arrival in each country, I first met with officials of the United Nations and local government agencies affiliated with development programs or with family-planning efforts. A second series of meetings was held with leaders of women's organizations and with individual women known locally for their independent thinking. Based upon the recommendations of all these persons, field trips were organized. I made a concentrated effort to avoid show-case locales. Instead I stubbornly journeyed to those areas judged "not worth your time".

By train, bus, car, and most often Land-Rover, I traveled with a series of patient women interpreters, who were selected for their knowledge of the local language and the fact that they were *not* from the area to be visited: women, I believed, would speak more freely if they were sure no one in the village would ever know what they said.

The greatest challenge lay in finding, or creating, the situations in which women would speak openly. I sought to find women in natural groups: gathering for a class, waiting at a health center, selling in the market, or working together in the fields. When we first met, I discussed the object of my visit, we exchanged stories, and got to know one another. As the women gained confidence, I would ask if anyone wished to pursue the conversation in private. Usually, there was a surplus of volunteers.

These individual discussions covered a wide range of subjects. Each conversation commenced with a discussion of the changes that have taken place in peoples' lives in the last generation or two. After giving examples of "what it was like before" and "how it is now", each woman described the factors bringing change—good or bad—into her life. A myriad of subjects emerged: housing, food, alcoholism, politics, male-female relationships, children, love, disappointment,—and family planning.[2] To avoid giving the impression that I had a particular interest in the latter subject, I made no reference to family planning unless it was mentioned by my partner in dialogue.

The average conversation took well over an hour; some 150 conversations were recorded. The format of this report does not permit the publication of conversations in their entirety, nor even excerpts from all 150 discussions. Included are those conversations or parts of conversations that seem to me to best reflect views held by many women, in many cultures, in the six countries I visited. Each conversation has been edited to include only the portions pertinent to attitudes on family planning or the issue that everywhere emerged as key—that of personal autonomy. In the interest of brevity, I have shortened the questions and have sometimes combined, in one reply, answers to several questions. The translated conversations have been edited as necessary for comprehension and to protect the privacy of individuals.

I told the women I talked to that I had come to record their views because people concerned with the status and the advancement of women everywhere in the world were anxious to learn what was going on in their lives. Reassured by a promise of anonymity, they seized the opportunity to send a message, "to talk back", as some said.

[2]An analysis of the interviews entitled, "Third World Women Speak Out: Interviews in Six Developing Countries" will be published by the Overseas Development Council in the spring of 1978.

Illiterate or inexperienced as many of them were, the views of these women on the changes they perceive, the needs for our common future, and the values that must be dominant, speak well for the dignity of the human spirit.

The long hours of individual conversations brought laughter and, sometimes, tears. I was asked about my "bride price", the "food you eat", "how men treat women in your place". I was asked for help I could not give and for advice I dared not give.

Sharing each other's experiences, we became help-mates and friends, learning from each other. They were reaching out for knowledge. But so was I. I left each woman with a sense of regret. There was never enough time. . . .

The message they send is urgent.

Perdita Huston
September, 1977

I CHANGE, NEEDS, CHOICE

> *"If a woman could start from the
> beginning to make her husband
> understand that she has rights just as he
> has rights . . . it would be different.
> Women must be taught this. They must
> learn that they, too, have rights . . ."*
> Zahia Marzouk[1]

How is one to understand a woman's attitudes—any woman's—on such a personal issue as the planning of births in her family without first delving into the reality of her life? What is the situation in which she lives? What is the range of her freedom to make decisions? What are the burdens she bears, in numbers of children already born to her or in the tasks she must perform?

These questions apply to women in New York City as they do to the 150 women in remote villages of the developing world who contributed to this report. True, their answers will vary. But all will speak to a part or to the whole of this trinity: change, needs, choice.

CHANGE

For most of the women I encountered, change—whether seen in their lifetime, or as compared to the lives of their mothers—seems to hold a negative connotation. In their mothers' time, most of them said, "life was not as difficult" or "as complicated". "Now we have to have cash to live." "We have less to eat than before." Some women acknowledged that

[1]President, Family Planning Association of Alexandria, interviewed June 1, 1976, Alexandria.

1

modern roads, electricity, water supply—to the extent that they exist—have simplified their lives. But the dominant change mentioned was in their economic situation, and this, they said, "is not good".

They did name, of course, several positive elements of change. Education was chief among these. Their mothers, for the most part, had been illiterate. Once schools were too far, too costly, or "girls just didn't go to school in those days". Today schools are more accessible; most children are permitted to attend at least through the primary grades. In general these women view education as the key to progress and to a better economic situation for the entire family—daughters and sons—though I met some who said their sons were attending school but it "was best that the daughters stay at home to help", as have generations of young girls before them. Most intend to do everything possible to educate their children. I met illiterate peasant women who had created cooperative markets for the sole purpose of raising money for their children's school fees.

Surprisingly, few women mentioned improved health-care as a change in their environment, even though health-care services have been made available in most areas only within the last generation. Already, they seemed to take this change for granted.

The new mobility of women, the freedom to move about and talk with one another and with other tribes, seems to be a considerable improvement in the lives of some. The freedom to choose one's husband, or at least to have veto power over the family's choice, is also welcomed as a formidable victory over the tradition-bound past. Only a very few women appeared to be resigned to the fact that they had "been married off" or that, eventually, they would be "given away to some unknown man".

Conversely, one change mentioned repeatedly and with distress, regardless of country or ethnic or religious identification, was the disintegration of relationships between men and women. Over and over again I was told: "Men were better in the old times; they took care of their families"; "There is no trust between men and women anymore". Older women complained about the lack of communication with their menfolk. Unmarried girls voiced the hope that their husbands would "talk with me", "plan with me", or "be understanding" and spoke of their fear that communication between husband and wife is rare, if not downright impossible.

NEEDS

When the women I interviewed expressed needs, access to training for themselves as well as to formal education for their children ranked very high. "Women need to learn skills by which to earn money to feed their families." "They need to learn agricultural techniques to improve crops and the family food supply." "They should learn sewing or handicrafts." One woman stressed that women need to learn simple notions of accounting and marketing. In the poorer areas, women spoke also of the need for improved health-care and nutrition and hygiene education, but even here the emphasis was on being taught how to do it themselves.

Asked what it is they would have liked to learn if they had been able to attend school, most women mentioned the skills necessary for occupations that serve others in the community: teacher, social worker, doctor, midwife, a women's group leader. I was repeatedly moved by the expressions of this wish to be useful to others coming from women who struggle daily for survival. Yet service to others did not appear to be associated with political activities. Virtually no one mentioned political leaders as role models for themselves or their children.

When questioned about the equality of men and women who had received equivalent education, women consistently replied: "Yes, women are equal to men." "Boys and girls, if they have the same chances, are the same." "Yes, I would vote for a woman for Parliament." But when it came to their own participation in local affairs, like a chorus these women replied: "It is not for me." "You have to be tough." "You have to be strong for you will be insulted and ridiculed." And, most women added: "Besides, my husband would never permit it." Many openly stated that women should not go into politics, explaining: "It is a dirty game", or "not a woman's place". Although women's groups often initiate policy within the village, their members rarely relate this type of community involvement to the political process at large.

When asked what they would do for women if they were

head of the country, women's replies again were education-oriented: "Help them become educated." "Teach them hygiene." "Teach them how to raise their children." "I would help the poor; I would give them work and houses." Very seldom did they mention the need for legal reform. There was little knowledge of the legal status of women; only a few stated that they would change the laws to improve the lot of women. Also, I found scant awareness of women leaders in government or national organizations. Some women could name the president's wife or the leader of a local women's organization. Only a handful could remember the names of women leaders outside their immediate area.

Rural women were surprisingly generous in their judgements of those in power. When asked, for example, if they thought their leaders (or the politicians) were responsive to women's needs, the answer was usually affirmative.

The more educated women, however, accused government of paying "lip service only" to women's involvement in nation building. Several governments, following International Women's Year, had set up a Women's Bureau, or a special office, to ascertain and respond to the needs of women in their country. But little was accomplished. "When women do acquire certain rights, the leaders do not inform them about it," many said. "Leaders are not guiding us; they don't really care about us."

Tunisia, where nearly every woman I met mentioned President Habib Bourguiba's effort to help women and to involve them in national life, was the exception to such criticisms. Even nomad women in remote areas of Tunisia referred to the law of 1956 that gave them equal status with men. This is not surprising, since President Bourguiba has associated the advancement of women with his nation's over all development plan for more than 20 years.

CHOICE

When it came to choice, the intensity of emotion in the replies to my questions constantly troubled me. As a means of measuring women's perception of themselves, their status and roles, I often asked whether or not there had been a time in their lives when they had thought it better to be a man. Although the better-educated women protested, "No, I am happy to be a woman", and some felt that being a woman is best because "women take better care of their families than do men", they admitted nonetheless that men have more choice in their lives. The poorer and illiterate women confessed they had often wished to be men "to be free to study, to learn and to work", "so I could choose whom I would marry". "Men look down on us and think we are not capable." One woman softly observed, "I would have liked to be born a man so as to care for my family and my wife." Her husband, unashamedly, had abandoned her and their five children.

In the more remote regions, women condemned traditions that still limit the freedom of women to move about. "People should realize that women need to come and go, to participate, just as men do." They felt closed off from the world and were eager to seek knowledge about, and from, other women.

But everywhere, the major advantage of being a man was seen to be more access to education. Many women told of brothers who went to school while they were kept at home. "My father said: 'Girls don't need to be educated'."

These women did not object to their state of femaleness; they resented only their inferior roles, their inability to partake of life more fully, their lack of choice. They seek participation and self-determination.

When I asked a woman, who it was that influenced her more in her childhood, her mother or father, I usually got one of two types of replies. If she was in a slight way different from her peer group (because she had gone to school for a time or had learned some useful skill), most said it was due to the fact that her father had encouraged her: "My father said I could do anything if I wanted it badly enough"; or "My father had all the influence in the family. He wanted me to learn a skill." Illiterate and unskilled women most frequently gave the opposite answer: "My father and brothers wouldn't let me go out of the house once I became ten years old"; or "My father wanted me to stay in the kitchen."

When I asked what they sought as qualities in a spouse, women answered: "A man who will give me freedom to learn and to move about." "A man who cares for his family." "One who will talk with me so we can plan together for the future."

To a Westerner, the desire to plan together seems almost superfluous; we assume that is what marriage is all about. But most of the women I talked with felt shut out of a participatory role within their marriages and described their situation as one of toil, submission, and resignation.

How do these briefly sketched reactions to change, expressions of needs, and deeply felt views of choice, affect attitudes to family planning, or the ability of women to make use of its availability?

THE MALE ROLE

Under olive trees in Tunisia, beside tea bushes in Sri Lanka, or in the cattle fields of Kenya, rural women expressed the same longing: "I don't want to have many children. I want to give those I have a better life than mine." *But:* "My husband would go off and marry another woman if I don't have a child every year." "My husband says the more children he has, the more prestige he will have." "I don't dare discuss it with my husband."

The women making these comments claimed that they themselves want to use some form of contraception but are not free to do so. Of the women who did practice family planning, the great majority had the consent of their husbands. The inescapable assumption is that when the husband is informed and supportive, a woman is more apt to use a contraceptive method.

Yet, in every country I visited, family planning personnel stressed that not enough is being done to inform men of their programs. A medical doctor in the Sudan advised, "Family planning programs should be aimed *especially* at men. Women come to see us and want to plan their families; then they return home and the husband says "No". Others say that men are afraid that their wives might "go bad" and become prostitutes if they are allowed to use contraceptives. The director of a regional office of the Family Planning Association of Kenya said: "There is such poor communication between the husband and the wife that it is necessary to convince the men of the usefulness of family planning. We have left the men out," he admitted, "and it is a problem."

Whether they use a contraceptive method or not, most women I met have heard about family planning and could name one or two methods of contraception. The source of their information was mostly word of mouth: from a friend or a family member. Other sources named were medical personnel, social workers, or women's organizations. The media, especially the radio, which might provide family planning information, were rarely mentioned—and are not in many areas, widely utilized for this seemingly obvious purpose.

A survey of a small village in the Gezira province of the Sudan revealed that of the women living in that semi rural area who knew about family planning, 75 percent had heard about it from other women, friends, or family.[2]

Asked if the women of her village discussed family planning together, a 45-year old Tunisian replied, "Of course. That's all we talk about."

This talking together has some drawbacks. Everywhere I traveled the directors of family planning programs told tales of rumors that hinder acceptance of contraceptive methods. "Once you take the pill you will become sterile. Don't believe that it is just temporary." "Pills produce deformed children." In Kenya, the current rumor was about "a woman who got sick and had to be operated on. They opened her brain and found her IUD."

Given the complaints women voice about contraceptive methods they use or have tried, it is understandable that wild rumors come to exist, ("pills made me sick", "the IUD made me bleed a lot and I'm anemic now"—dizziness, bleeding, backaches, headaches). Once they tell each other of their symptoms, a potential rumor is loosed. Only a handful of women told me, "I am fine".

The damage these complaints and resultant rumors can do to family planning programs is evidenced in the Arbagi village report quoted above. Of those who refused to plan their families, 37 percent said it was "because of the danger to the mother's health". In Sri Lanka, the major fear was cancer. The only method about which I heard no complaint was the tubectomy but, then again, I did not meet many women who had undergone permanent sterilization.

In areas where cultural taboos and superstition are a very real part of people's lives I found that, although women were sometimes suspicious of modern methods of contraception,

[2]Sudan Family Planning Association: *A Family Planning Survey of Arbaji Village in Gezira Area*, Sudan, 1973.

traditional methods were still in use. When asked if they knew of, or had ever practiced, any "old way" of contraception, many replied affirmatively. Some described the use of a sort of aspirin in the vagina to prevent conception. Sri Lankans sometimes rely on charmed coconuts and other talismen. In Egypt women place cotton, saturated with oil, in the vagina prior to having sexual relations — a centuries-old contraceptive method. Some told of swallowing mothballs and then laughed at their foolishness. One Tunisian woman, now using a modern contraceptive, referred to the making of a preventative pill consisting of a dried umbilical cord from the last-born child, ground meal, and cows' urine. "Oh yes," she laughed. "We were so ignorant before. We did those things and they never worked."

Far back into history women have sought ways, often harmful to their health, to limit the number of children they bear. But there is a major difference between the strange potions, or more often the furtive abortions of the old days and modern contraceptive methods. Traditional methods can be used in secret. The husbands never find out about "the old ways" because they don't involve going to a clinic. Mexico provides an example: although family planning services are available in most areas of the country, the National Population Council estimates that over 1 million "home-made" abortions are performed each year. Women have only to explain to their husbands that they are "having some sort of female sickness", and the subject is not mentioned again.

In starting out on the journey described in chapters that follow, I had my own thoughts about possible answers to the questions posed by less-than-successful population program efforts. In my experience in one village years ago, I had observed that women had little or no power of decision in their lives. Their menfolk made almost every decision concerning family life and the lives of girls and women.

But this had been only a single, personal observation, some years back. Would it prove to be true today in other villages and in other countries? If so, perhaps it might follow that when women have the support and understanding of their men, they are more free to partake of family planning services.

II KENYA

*"Family planning is not for one member
of the family only . . . not just the woman.
Men ought to be taught about it but
communications methods which reach
the men are few and very ineffective."*

Maggie Gona[1]

Just a few short years ago, Nairobi was a peaceful capital
city, its shape recognizable, its rate of growth slow. The Nairobi
of 1976 is a different place, its pace of change all too rapid.

Capital investment and "development" have brought great
wealth to some, while impoverishing others, and have caused
uncontrolled urban pull that has changed the nation's social
structures dramatically. Youth is caught between traditional
family conduct and wholesale acceptance of values and ideas
from abroad. This dilemma takes on added importance when
one learns that 55 percent of the population of Kenya is under 20
years of age.

Eighty percent of Kenya's surface has been classified as
arid or marginal land. Eighty percent of the nearly 13 million
people live from agriculture. Due to migration, death, desertion,
or polygamy, one-third of all rural households are headed by
women. These women produce 80 percent of the foodstuffs
consumed by Kenyan families.

In the past several years, Kenya has suffered prolonged
drought. Over and over in remote areas I heard the explanation
for poor health or nutrition as "the rains have failed us again".
Yet, due to its expanding economy, Kenya is far better off than

[1]Chairperson, Family Planning Association of Kenya, Mombasa Chapter,
interviewed July, 1976, Mombasa.

most developing nations. But how does its economic boom affect rural women? Quite simply, they work harder than before for little or no reward.

On the small roads leading to market, one meets the typical Kenyan woman. She is tall and handsome. She carries a baby on her back while balancing an enormous market basket of vegetables on her head. Her eyes are lowered to watch her hands weaving another basket she hopes to sell when she reaches the market. It will help pay the school fees of that 7-year-old who is walking behind her. Never in Kenya did I observe a rural woman at rest. She is always busy, always at work.

As men enter into salaried employment, women remain on the family plot of land to scratch out a living for themselves and their children. When they have moved to the cities with their husbands and into the high-rise buildings, Dr. Julia Ojiambo, Assistant Minister for Housing and Social Welfare, says, "They find nothing more than a place for people to commit suicide. Kenyans like to be on the ground; they like to have a piece of soil to call their own." In most cases women remain on the land and take on the tasks of weeding, sowing, reaping, storing. The economic and social gap between husband and wife widens.

In Nairobi, women leaders, both in and outside official organizations, spoke of the plight of their rural sisters. "Do not listen to me. You must go to the rural areas if you want to understand what is happening in Kenya today." And it is true. In the fields, in schoolhouses, or in the mud huts most families call home, women told me of what they have experienced and observed. They spoke first of change; it has not been good.

M'BALE VILLAGE

We arrived in the clearing occupied by four round thatch-roofed huts in mid-afternoon. I had been told that most of the young people had left the village to seek work or better conditions elsewhere. Waiting for us was a group of some 30 elderly members of the Luo tribe, men to one side, women to the other. My interpreter and I greeted each one individually, then took our place in a circle.

We told of the object of my visit, talked about crops and rain, answered questions, asked about women's work and the change in women's lives. A bit later, I asked if the men would excuse us so that we might go into one of the homes for more "women talk." Everyone laughed, playfully, and permission was granted.

In a windowless room, lighted only by the open door, we sat on stools or on the floor. The atmosphere was cheerful and relaxed. The 14 M'Bale women seemed happy to have a visitor "for themselves alone." Through the interpreter, I began:

    — I understand you have formed a cooperative here. What are the plans?
    = We have started a group and are trying to put up a building for adult education and handicrafts. You can see the tracing for the foundation on the ground outside. We are all women and we are trying to get money, but we haven't got enough yet to keep our work going. We are having money problems.

The woman who spoke was undoubtedly the eldest of the group. A large round-faced woman, wearing a cotton dress covered by a heavy hand-knit sweater as protection against the crisp winter air, with her grey hair covered with a kerchief tied at the back of her neck, she smiled constantly, fully enjoying her elder status.

"Can you ask her how old she is?" I addressed the interpreter.

"She says she doesn't know," came the reply as the room filled with laughter and the interpreter turned to me and added, "She says she was born a long time ago. All she remembers is that she was married about the time of the First World War."

"So that would make her at least 75 years old. Ask her to tell me what it was like in those days."

    — How was it different then from today?
    = That is a difficult question. We lived all right, happily. In those days things were quite different. We were walking naked. We had no clothing. We started wearing clothing not long ago. We used to just wear something to cover this part only.

The old woman pointed to her pelvis.

= They were made from banana fiber. We would feel the cold but we were used to it.

She paused, looked around, then said slowly:

= And in those days we mixed more freely with men—there was no difference between us, and we trusted each other.
− What do you mean by that? Please explain.
= Now, in these times, there is no trust. They [men] are not straight-forward people. These are the changes.

Another woman took up the comparison, saying,

= We had goats, cows, sheep, and hens. Even chickens never got sick in those days, they never died. But we had no hospitals, and if we were sick, and if we knew any medicine or any herbs, we used them.
− Did many women have trouble during childbirth?
= They used to have problems but there were some old women who knew herbs and that helped them. But there were problems.
− What was the traditional way of meeting a husband?
= A relative would tell the girl that she knew a good boy, then the relative would come to the family and they would agree together. Then the boy would see her and agree, and his family would agree. The boy paid three cows, two goats, and they were married.
− Do you think people nowadays are as respectful of older family members as they used to be?
= There is change. People don't respect others as much anymore. We see things change but we don't know why they don't respect us.
− Does it have to do with the education of children?
= It is good to educate children because we want them to have an education and keep our country good. We want educated people so we can have good leadership.
− Do you think boys and girls should go to school?
= Yes, but it is better to educate a girl rather than a boy, although you should educate them both. The girl is better than the boy because girls help a lot. Even this house, my

daughter built it for us. If you don't have any daughters, who will build for you? The boys will marry and take care of their wives, that's all. They don't care about the mothers.
– Well, mothers raise the sons. Why aren't you teaching your boys to be responsible sons and husbands?
= We have tried this, but you know, men have big heads. They don't listen. They have defeated us.

I looked around the room at this point and realized that this subject was not altogether welcome. So I turned to the others and asked:

– Let's hear about how many children you have—around the room, one by one.
= Ten—one died, I have nine.
= I had nine, five died, now I have four.
= I had ten, two died.
= Eleven but two died.
= I had seven; one died.
= Nine; three died.
= Thirteen, but three died.
= Eleven—four died so I have only seven.
= I had eleven, too, but eight died. Now I have only three.
– What were all these deaths from?
= Mine, it was diarrhea.
= Two died from malaria.
= They died when they were still very young. In a short time, they died. I don't know why.
= I don't know, either. The child complained, fell sick, and was dead.
= It is because in those days we had no hospitals nearby. These days we have got doctors and hospitals, and therefore the children are treated. They don't die like before.
– Let's go around again. Since you say that children don't die as often as before, tell me how many children you think is a good number for a family today.
= Four.
= Six.
= Four.
= Ten and more.
= Four.

= Six.

= It's better to have five and have them all grow.

= Four, because of education.

= A long time ago, in those days, even ten was good. Now, if there are four, that is enough.

= In the olden days when they used to have ten or eight children, we were happy because we had many girls and boys to be married and get children so we would have more grandchildren. Now I would like to have only four.

− In some countries I have visited, women have told me of traditional ways to limit the number of children. Was there any such thing here?

= If someone wanted to not have many children, pressure from all the other people would do.[2] What they used to do was every time you gave birth your mother came and shook your hand and said, "My daughter, don't produce every year, have spacing. Let your children be spaced."

Another woman wanted to add her own story.

= Even if you had ten, during those days, you could care for them all. I used to have children this high—the speaker held her hand level with her waist—before I would have another. I used only my menstruation period. While nursing, I would take a long time to get my menstruation.

− How long did you nurse your children?

= Eight months.

= A year.

= Eight months.

= Two years.

= A year.

− Does anyone know other ways besides lactation to limit the number of children?

The interpreter paused to listen to them, all talking at once,

[2]Author's note: In some polygamous tribes of Kenya, it wasn't considered well-mannered to give birth too frequently. Abstinence was practiced until the last child became old enough to walk and talk. At that point the mother would send a "message," usually in the form of an object, delivered to the father's hut by the child. When the husband received the gift, he knew that he could now visit that wife once again.

then she leaned over to explain, "This one is giving the right answer but I think the name is difficult for her. She says when people go to school and they go away, they've got something that they put inside."

"Have the others heard about this?"

"Yes, this one says there is something they can insert inside that prevents conceiving but it brings disease—it will make you sick and you won't get any more children."

This comment prompted a long discussion about "new methods" and questions about my own family. Had I planned my family, how old were my children, and so on? I ended the group discussion by asking:

— What do you think women here need most in order to have a better situation, a better life?

= We need teachers.

= Yes, we need teachers who will teach women about sewing and weaving.

= And agriculture.

= And someone to help us sell the things we make.

= You see, we want to build this adult center so we can learn weaving and crafts, to sell. Nobody will come to teach us unless we have a proper place. What we need is teachers.

— And what about the radio? Do you have the opportunity to listen to the radio? Does it help you learn new things?

= One family has a radio. We like to hear news and agricultural programs.

The interpreter repeated again, "Yes, that is what each one is saying. They're interested in news and agricultural lessons."

— Do you hear any news about women on the radio?

= No.

A SUGAR BELT COOPERATIVE FARM

It took over an hour to drive out to the central office of the cooperative, and then on through the fields to a settlement hidden in the tall cane stalks. The mud huts were well spaced, far from one another, but small and in need of repair. The one large building made of sod bricks was rectangular and had a tin roof.

I was told that this building had been constructed within the past months, following an outbreak of cholera. Many had died, and a doctor had been sent to help the survivors improve the latrines and the village water supply. At his insistence, the building had been erected to provide shelter for his medical consultations and for group meetings. The social worker traveling with me told me the settlement was "too remote for visits from the Family Planning field workers." Only since the outbreak of cholera had it received regular attention from government services.

The crowd gathered around us — women of all ages, infants and children, nearly 40 people in all. We entered the new building and found that it was cool inside. The shutters were but half open and the quiet semi-darkness seemed to give confidence to the more timid among us. The discussion became a group affair quickly. We learned that no women in the village had ever been to school. Only a few had traveled outside the plantation. Only one family had a radio.

The first woman to be interviewed privately had lived on the settlement for 32 years. She thought she was about 49 years old. She had seven children.

    — Can you tell us what differences you see between your life and that of your mother and grandmother?

    = Life is more difficult now. One of the things is that we didn't have to spend very much money before. When you went on a journey you just walked and you didn't have to have clothes. But now you can't do anything without using money. That's one of the difficulties.

    — Did your mother farm the land as you do? What crops do you raise?

    = My mother was like me. I raise a bit of corn, some beans, groundnuts, and sweet potatoes. I buy the vegetables I don't grow and some meat.

    — How do you earn the money you need?

    = I trade. I sell parts of my crops here on the settlement and some of it I have to take to market and sell it there.

    — Is your life easier or more difficult than your mother's?

    = It is more difficult.

– Do your children go to school?

= My sons are still in school but my daughters didn't go because I couldn't raise the money to send them. The boys are younger so I had time to prepare. I would like one of them to be an engineer and another to be a teacher. The girls are both married now.

– At what age did they marry, and how many children do they have?

= One at 16, one 17, and the other at 15. The eldest has four children and the other one two. The last one has just one child but is expecting another.

– Does the one with three want more children?

= I can't answer that question. I do not know how she feels about it. We don't talk to each other about such things.

– Do you know of any way of limiting the number of births in the family?

= The only method I know is the old native way. They used to use some herbs that would sort of control it. They used to boil the herbs and drink them. They still use them . . . and it works.

– What are these herbs called?

= I don't know. There are certain people who know these herbs. I don't know how to identify them, and I don't even know their names. I never used such things.

– What do you think the women in this settlement need most to improve their lives?

= Food. They need more food for themselves instead of having to sell it for cash. They need to know more about agriculture so they can raise better crops.

– What about their families? What do you think is the ideal number of children per family?

= Three or four at the most. (She has seven.)

– If a man and a woman have the same education, do you see any difference in their ability? Tell me what you think about this.

= If they could have equal chances at education and training, I don't see any difference between the two.

– Has there been a time in your life when you thought it would be better to have been born a boy?

= Even now there are times when I wish I had been born a man instead of a woman because women have a lot of problems. Sometimes if you get married to a drunkard he goes out, he drinks, he doesn't even care what you are going to eat with the children in the house. Due to that, even if you were doing some sort of trade or have a small income, it isn't adequate because you have children and you have to buy clothes for them and food and pay for school fees. There are quite a number of women who have such husbands and, therefore, have a lot of difficulties in life. We have just a few who lead a good life.

We talked a bit more in this vein and then I asked if there were any questions the woman who had been speaking would like to ask me in return. She smiled. Straightening out the folds of her skirt nervously, she raised her eyes to mine. The interpreter translated: "She says she has one question she would like to ask you. What do you think you would do if you had a husband who was always drunk and didn't help?" This was not the first time that I had been asked such a question and I found no answer.

Anxious to understand what a younger woman of this settlement might say about change in her life, I spoke next with a 17-year-old who had been married for a year but had no children as yet.

— Do you see any difference between your life and your mother's?
= There is no difference.
— And with your grandmother's life?
= With my grandmother there's a difference but with my mother it is almost the same. One of the differences from my grandmother . . . there was a better understanding between them and their husbands than there is now, between the younger generation. I think men have changed.
— Do you have any idea why? What has changed them?
= It is the kinds of lives people are leading now. That is the change.
— What do men do now that makes them different from before?
= These days the husband is always looking for too many

little problems. They're always trying to supervise and find fault with their wives. That makes room for many quarrels.
 — What happens here when a husband beats his wife?
 = Even if you are beaten, nothing happens. It is between you and your husband, and the rest of the members of the family.
 — Do you have any idea how many children you would like to have?
 = Four. These days there are very many difficulties. If I have four, I will have fewer difficulties.
 — But you are very young. You can have many, many children. How are you going to manage to have just four?
 = I don't know any way. I would like to have some control so that I get only four children. I don't want more than that.
 — And what do you want most for your children?
 = Education. I would like them to get enough education.
 — And you, if you had a chance to learn something new, what would you like most to learn?
 = I would like to be a nurse; I would treat people.
 — Do you think men have more choices in life than women?
 = I think women have the chance of doing more things than men. It is only that men's chances are better recognized because they only concentrate on a few things. Women have got so many things to do that nobody ever looks at how much they do.
 — Do you think it would be better if you had been born a man?
 = Never. I never wished to be a man.

GIRLS' TRAINING CENTER, WESTERN KENYA

Several miles from Nakuru, a colonial plantation home converted into a training center for young girls dominates a vast sloping valley. Its grounds are well kept and maintained in a formal colonial style. Our meeting took place in a high-ceilinged room that probably had served as the salon in British times. There was no heating. The day was cold, and we warmed our hands by rubbing them together constantly as we talked.
 The first volunteer for a personal interview was 19 years old and training to become a nursery school teacher. She had come

to this remote institution from her native province a hundred miles away. She spoke openly, though hesitantly, needing constant reassurance from the interpreter. As we talked, the sun began to set. A young girl brought us a gas lamp. It warmed us more than it lit the room.

— Tell me about yourself and your family.

= We are a family of seven children. I don't have any religious training, but I am a Protestant. I was a student, but due to financial difficulties I had to stop. That is why I wanted to join this course. I was just staying at home. I am not sure I will have work in my town when I finish, but I would be willing to go to another town. I have applied to a nursery school in Nairobi. I would like that.

— Given what you know about the women in your home area, what do you think they need most to know or learn to improve their lives?

= Women around Nyeri need education—education on nutrition because some children are ill fed. When I went back there to do my field work for this course, I saw cases of marasmus and kwashiorkor.[3] I had to stop teaching the children and start educating the parents. The parents needed advice on home life.

— You told me you have a fiance. Tell me what you believe to be the ideal qualities in a husband.

= I would like all husbands to spare time to stay at home because it is very common, especially in Nyeri, that men do not spend time at home. The children sometimes don't know their fathers. Their fathers come home during the night and go in the morning. They have no time to see their children. I would like them to be sympathetic to their wives. You see, our men take many wives so that the wives will do everything for the family, then the husband won't have to work hard.

— Do you have any idea of how many children you would like to have once you are married?

= Yes, I want to have four children because I don't think this day-care-center job can make enough money to support more than four. I will ask advice from the midwife in

[3]Deficiency diseases caused by malnutrition.

the clinic, then I will try to use some family planning method.

– How did you first hear about family planning?

= I heard it on a radio program which comes every evening from a doctor at the hospital. I have many women friends, and they always advise me. One women here has a coil.

– What do you think is the importance of planning one's family?

= First of all, I don't blame my parents but—when I was studying, I always thought that if there were no children following me perhaps I could have continued my education. When I left school I was in despair. Also, for me, the reason for family planning is to give my children a good education, for my health and for the health of my family too.

– When you have your children, what do you want most for them?

= First of all, I would like them to get a lot of love from good parents. If I get married, I would like them to get that from me and my husband. When they go to school, I would like them to continue, not only education but technical skills also.

– You mentioned the radio. Tell me what kinds of programs you prefer.

= I like the one which the doctor does and the news. I like to hear about what is going on in politics.

– Politics? Have you heard of any women in politics here? Do you think women make as effective leaders as men?

= There are several women in Parliament, Dr. Julia Ojiambo, for example. And women are leading even in a better way than men because you can find, especially in my area, that our big projects are mostly depending upon women rather than men. I don't know why men don't like it, but now women seem to be taking over the old work of men.

Watching my reaction, she continued:

= Women are starting now to fight for their places in local councils and Parliament, and they are defeating men. You find that after the election men are surprised to discover that women have won. I don't know, they have got that hatred in their hearts. They don't like to be surpassed by women, especially Africans. It is very strong here because if a woman has a husband who should not do something, something very bad, he will do it because a woman told him not to. He wants to prove himself by doing it.

Men must be taught that we are human beings like them, and must lead human lives like them—I don't know why they don't regard us as people.

VIHIGA DISTRICT

Most of the women who were to meet us in the empty wooden primary school were of the Luhya tribe, a farming tribe that struggles to scratch a livelihood from the rocky soil in this densely populated area. The schoolhouse stood in a large field. Children were playing at a distance and we could hear their voices ringing across the meadow-like play area. A few older children gathered around us to catch a glimpse of "the visitor". But as we entered the schoolhouse to sit on rough wooden benches, to share again tales of change and life's ways, a tiny elderly woman made sure there were no curious children within earshot.

The woman recorded here was married at age 18 and is now 35 years old. She looked much older and seldom smiled. Her front bottom teeth were missing. Many Luhya tribe members have had their teeth extracted as a precaution against a disease that locks the jaw and prevents its victim from eating or drinking. Teeth are still removed systematically "just in case" this disease strikes again.

– Tell me about your family. How many children do you have?
= I had eight, two died, so I now have six.
– How did they die? At birth? Of disease?
= One died when she was six, the other at two. They were sick only a few days. When I took them to the hospital they couldn't survive. I think they died from measles.
– How old is your youngest child?
= Three years.
– Can you tell me the differences you see in your life as compared to the life of your mother or grandmother?

= My grandmother and my mother used to eat differently. You know, we have got some small animals that look something like rats. They used to be eaten in the old days. My grandmother was one of those who used to eat the small animals. My mother used to eat a type of vegetable which grows even in the bush just like spinach. So you see, there were differences because they ate different kinds of things. And our mothers didn't have any clothes. They gave birth to about ten, twelve, or fourteen children. These days you find that people have got only two, some have got three, because of giving them proper education, feeding them properly, and these days the cost of living is going too high.

She hesitated for a moment, then went on . . .

= When you give birth to children every year it is no good because the children are not going to have good health, and then the people will say, "Look at this one who does not know how the world is changing." If you have two children, you have got two eggs to give to those two children. That is much better than having two eggs and eight children.
− I agree, but do you know how women are having less children than in the past?

The interpreter listened carefully and said, "She's trying to think of the name which is dealing with that sort of thing." After a moment of hesitation, the interpreter added, "Yes, she knows about family planning."

− If you had known about family planning before you had eight children, what size family would you want to have?
= When I heard about it I really wanted to find out where it was available. Many of us have gone into that. I am taking the injection.
− Do you have any side effects from it?
= No, I'm fine.
− Let's talk about the women here in this village. What do you think they need most?
= Teachers from the outside to help us with crafts, nutrition, and agriculture or about the family. My problem is my husband. If only men can be taught to look after their

families. My husband is working far from here and he does not send any money, so if these sorts of things are taught, telling them to take care of their family, this would be of great help.

  — Was it the same with your father and grandfather or is this another change?

= This is the change we have now, not in the olden days.

— Is there any reason for this change?

= I think it is because of too much drinking, and, therefore, their minds do not think far.

— Did you ever go to school?

= No, but now I am learning to read and write in the adult literacy class.

— If you had been able to go to school, is there any profession you would have liked to learn?

= Teaching.

— And what about your children? Do they go to school?

= Four of them are going to school, one girl is married, a boy is working in Nairobi, but four are in school.

— Do you think that when boys and girls have the same education they are the same?

= Girls are good. They will help you more than boys. I am educating them all because if you leave a boy out, and he's the one you're going to stay with the rest of your life, you may have troubles with him, so it is better to educate them all. But the girls are of greater help. They care more about the family than do the boys.

Until now, this worn, emaciated woman before me had been shy and hesitant. With these last questions, she began to look me in the eye, searching perhaps for my understanding of what it is like to be alone, digging in the family plot, fending for six children, and trying to earn enough to send four of them to school. We talked quietly awhile of children, both hers and mine. Later, when she seemed more composed, I asked:

  — What do you think is the greatest change you've seen in your life?

= God is helping me. He is helping me use my hands to make handicrafts, mats, baskets and dolls. With this I can get a bit of money for the school fees.

- Do you ever have a chance to listen to the radio? What do you like to hear?
= I don't have a radio but a friend does. I like to listen to family planning programs, to talks on agriculture, and to the news.

This Vihiga District woman could not name any women in "the news." She believes it is good for women to be involved in community affairs or in politics, and she said she would vote for a woman candidate. She did not know what happens when a man divorced his wife.

- If you were ever the president of this country, what would you do for women?
= I would give them employment, something by which they could live—increase the salaries for those who are working. For those who are at home on small farms, the price of grains should be increased so that they can feed their families.
- Now a last question: Was there ever a time when you wished you had been born a boy?
= Yes. My mother had 13 children, all daughters, so I used to think, "I wish God had made me a boy". And even up to now, when I go to our home I always feel I wish God had made me a man. My father, whenever he sees me, he always says the same thing: "I wish this daughter of mine had been made a man".

MOMBASA

The changes brought about by Kenya's economic boom, so visible in Nairobi, seems on the surface not to have affected the Indian Ocean port city of Mombasa. A melange of African tribes, East Indians and Arabs stroll the city's commercial district. Moslem women shrouded in great heaps of heavy black cloth, only their feet and hands sometimes visible, can be seen walking together swiftly. Two or three miles west of them, in the rural areas, women wear only a *fouta* draped around their hips.

But when a group of 12 women representing the major women's groups of the Mombasa district met with us one morning (religious organizations, self-help groups, market cooperatives, and service groups were represented), our conversation touched upon a variety of changes.

= There have been many, in the past generation. Here in Mombasa, for example, we have Moslems and Christians. Before, these people were separated. With social change we see that a Moslem girl will get married to a Christian boy. Moslem girls are going to school; they are working. But at the same time, control of the family is relaxing; it is not as tight as before. And you find that people don't like it very much. A big problem is to get the old people to understand that their lives have changed now.

These women also discussed their needs, some of them occasioned by changing times, some the result of traditional practices:

= The most important need for women now is to budget, how to cook, yes, but certainly how to budget. Say a husband earns about 300 shillings [approximately $36 U.S.], and she comes to you and says, "I have a problem with my husband. He doesn't want to give me money. I want this and I want that," and then you look into it and you find that her problems are created because she has no idea how to budget.
= You know, another thing we need is markets. It is a custom here for people to marry many wives, and sometimes they cannot afford it. In that case the woman has to do something to raise the standard of living of the family. The women cannot go and work in the offices because they have never been to school. Maybe they could earn some living through selling things outside their homes, like frying fish or some kind of food. But they have to have a license and they cannot afford to buy a government license. Something ought to be done so that women could be given a chance because most of the time they are the providers.
    In the rural areas, the women have a *shamba*, a family plot of land, and they get their food from it. In town there are no *shambas*. If they try to do something, stitch or sew, they have no market. They don't bring the right thing needed in the market. I think women need to be educated in

marketing needs. Someone should first investigate the
market and then teach the women to make what is needed.
The leaders should be educated first on how to find a
market before you start a group to teach them skills. Also,
the markets are controlled by men. They go into the rural
area and they undercut the women by buying cheap. So our
women should be educated and become industrialists.

– What about health-care needs in this district?

= One of the big problems is the children of prostitutes. In
every country where there is a port you have this prostitution going on. Here in Mombasa most of the prostitutes
have babies, and they take them to old women and say they
will pay to raise them. They have the children but they don't
want them. So the rural woman cares for the child but no
one comes to give her money, so she begins just making
porridge and the child gets undernourished and then she
comes to the clinic and the social worker gets involved and
so on and so on.

– And the medical services haven't tried to teach the prostitutes about family planning?

The women seated around the table laughed at my sugges-
tion. They were uneasy talking about prostitution, and the very
idea that one could teach prostitutes something made them even
more uneasy. Finally one spoke up, suggesting:

= I think they do, but I think family planning is still a
problem in Kenya. It has not really caught on yet. It has not
yet come to the people. I can say there is a step forward, but
we haven't really come into it very much.

– Tell me why you think people are not accepting family
planning?

= Fear, I think. Some of them say, "If you take too much
of this medicine, you will become this or that." There are a
lot of fears, so they are not very sure yet. But gradually I
think it is catching on. It will take a little bit of time. The
Family Planning has got a lot of work to do.

– Is it women who are more resistant or men?

= The men couldn't care less. They don't worry. You'll
never see a man going to a family planning clinic. They are
not interested. Some, I think, would like to have more

children to keep the women at home. There is that tendency in the men, especially here on the coast, "Let a woman free, then she'd be going everywhere . . ." so she must have a child every year until she becomes old.

= But women should fight that! Why should we be subjected to childbearing so they can go gadding about?

− Well, the main object of family planning is not to stop having children but to give the woman a rest between one child and the other—a choice.

= But that's what the men don't understand.

= Women are really getting to understand it though. I think within five years all women will be in family planning. They understand. They see the problem because even the men, themselves, they're not the same. They don't care much about their children.

In fact, the men who earn more, they just go and have more women outside and forget about their wives. So you are the one to suffer. If anything, you are given just food and then you don't see the husband for four days. You have to suffer and cope. The children, they are sick or something, and the woman is there alone. Women are starting to realize, "Well, I might as well start planning my children because I am the one who is suffering." I think it is catching up.

= If you meet a man who has four wives, and you know those wives are all suffering, and you ask him, "Why? Why all this?" He will say, "It is allowed by my religion," or "It is approved by the law." So there are many children, and the salaries are poor.

− What about legal measures against men who abandon their children or who take so many wives that they can't afford to care for them?

= The problem here is not taken seriously in the government, and I think it is really time for women to voice this. It should be a law—one man, one woman. But, you see, *who* is going to voice that? We have more men than women in Parliament so that the women's voices are not heard, and those men in Parliament, each one has three wives so they wouldn't agree to that. There was a law that if you got a girl pregnant, you've got to maintain the child until it is an adult. They abolished the law because most of the fathers were Parliament leaders. So the men are really oppressing the women, honestly. The men in Kenya are oppressing the women so badly, and there is nobody to push them.

= You see, our men in Kenya are very jealous, and they are still very strong. They hate the idea that a woman can speak up, the idea that a woman can voice her opinion, because men are very selfish; they just think about themselves. They don't think about others. But I hope that one day we are going to be able to get our way. I know we'll do it—slowly, because the moment they stop oppressing women, I think women could really run the country much better than men.

III EGYPT

"We must have sex education here. Our women are very sensitive and you can't have family planning without sex education. They are shy. . . They cover their face if you talk about family planning. . ."

Dr. Nawal Es Saadawi[1]

Hot, dusty, overcrowded Cairo stretches along the Nile into which Egyptians and foreigners alike constantly gaze, as if to find refuge from the bustling city of 9 million people. Egypt is nearing a population of 40 million and has an annual growth rate of over 2 percent. Ninety-nine percent of all Egyptians live on only 3.5 percent of the land, the Nile Valley and its delta, creating a population density of 2,700 per square mile—one of the highest in the world.

Following the Census of 1960, the Arab Republic of Egypt became the first Arab country to promulgate a national population policy. Egypt's Supreme Council for Family Planning, now reorganized into the Supreme Council for Population and Family Planning, was created in 1965 as an interministerial agency that could coordinate and research both action and policy among the different government bureaus. But Egypt was hindered in the pursuit of a strong family planning program by the wars of 1967 and 1973. Priorities had to be turned to the defense of its territories and of its people. At present a Five-Year Plan covering the population growth needs of the nation is being considered.

Egyptian officials recognize that the country no longer

[1]Medical Doctor and author, interviewed June, 1976, Cairo.

30

lacks the financial means for family planning programs for there are many international agencies willing to provide funds for population activities. It is the lack of infrastructure and of medical and para-medical services in Egypt that, these officials believe, bars greater advances.

In conversations with the educated women of Egypt, I learned of another problem. Over and again, they mentioned religion as a factor hindering progress. They said that religious leaders confuse family planning efforts with the overall emancipation of women, and "though the religious leaders might accept the arguments for population control, they cannot for the life of them consent to the emancipation of women".

SAINJIN

Guided by the advice of several members of the Cairo Women's Association, a service organization active in women's programs for over 20 years, we had driven north out of Cairo early one morning to visit a village west of the Alexandria road. The town was small but its streets were well-kept, even prosperous looking—a village of shopkeepers, small landowners, and the laborers who work the landed families' fields. We drove directly to the adult education building to find 30 women, all veiled in black, crowded into a classroom for a lecture on nutrition. When told of the object of my visit, they appeared eager to listen and, later, to be heard.

The first young woman recorded was 17 years old, educated, and now attending a commercial school. But her attitudes were similar to those of young women we met who had no formal education at all.

— So you say you are in the second year of commercial school?
= Yes, I am learning typing; I take the train to school each day.
— Tell me about your mother's life. At what age did she marry? Did she choose her husband?
= My mother married at 15. She had three girls and two boys. She never went to school and was married in the traditional way, but I will not be like her. I am engaged already. The first day my fiancé came to ask for my hand, I

saw him. He comes to visit from time to time. My parents asked my opinion—whether or not I wanted him. If I hadn't, I would have refused. I think my parents would accept my refusal.

— What are the most important qualities in a husband?

= That he be a religious man, that he take care of his home and his children, that he take good care of his wife and pay attention to her, that he work well and serve his country.

— What does your future husband do for work?

= He has a commercial school diploma but is now in the army.

— Do you have any idea how many children you would like to have?

= One boy and one girl. Just two. I know about pills. I know all about that.

— Have you and your fiancé talked about the number of children you will have?

= No, we haven't talked about it yet. We are only recently affianced.

— But what if your husband wants 10 children?

= I wouldn't accept it. He is well-educated, well-mannered, and I am sure he won't ask for such a thing.

— How is your life different from the past generations?

= The most important change concerns children. My mother raised lots of children because in those days life was not costly and they could live well. I don't want to have more than two because now life is much more expensive. With just two, I will have enough to get by.

— When and how did you hear about family planning for the first time?

= Ten years ago. I heard people here in the village talking and then I heard it on the radio.

— Have you heard about women leaders on the radio? Can you name any women here in Egypt who help people or who are leaders?

= No, I can't name any. My only world is here in the village. There are good people here who help the poor. They are the people who set an example for me to imitate, for me and the others of the village.

— Tell me, was there ever any time when you wished you had been born a boy?

= Here in the village when girls finish school, we go back into the house and stay there. It is rare that we go out at all. But the boys, of course, they are free to go as they please. I would like to have been a boy so as to move about and go out of the house. I hope that my children will be educated and that they will have greater liberty to move about . . . more freedom.

− Since you are going to commercial school, do you plan to work once you are married?

= My fiancé wants me to continue to study, but he doesn't want me to work once we are married. I would like to work but he doesn't want it. He says, "If we are in need one day, you will work, but if we don't need it, you can't." I'm obliged to follow his wishes.

From those who had volunteered to speak with us, I chose next an older woman who had earlier sat next to me. Her arms beneath her black veil appeared white and frail. She said she was 66 years old, and she had raised four children alone because she had been widowed when the children were still young. Two other children had died in infancy. Today, she cares for a granddaughter whose mother died eight years ago.

− How did you raise four children on your own?

= I worked in the fields. The children are grown now. I have only the 13-year old granddaughter with me.

− Have you seen much change in the village over the past years?

= There is electricity now, lights. People are more civilized, more educated than before. There are a lot of people who have made money. There are rich and poor. There are some nice people who take care of the poor, but others profit from everybody. There are the clinics where women can go to have their babies. That, too, didn't exist before. We just had the babies at home, with a *matrone*.

When I was a young girl, there were schools but girls didn't go to them. Later, my daughters were able to go to school, all except the second daughter who was too pretty, so my brother-in-law, who looked after the family after my husband's death, said she couldn't continue to go to school. He was jealous. He didn't want her to go for fear people would see her. All the other children went.

Now with my granddaughter, I can barely find enough for us to eat. I am not able to send her to school. That is why I go to literacy classes; I have to help her and myself.

– What about her father, can't he be of help?

= Her father is no good. When my daughter gave birth to a girl, he left her and remarried. He said, "You had a daughter, I want a son." He left her and took another wife. When my daughter died, he never did anything for the child. He left her with me. That is why I am having such a difficult time.

My other daughter is 42 and lives in Cairo. She has nine children, four boys and five girls. I wish she hadn't any at all, but you can't remain without some. She is too tired with all these children. When I go to visit her, I can't stay. There is too much trouble and confusion.

– Does your daughter want to have more children?

= She has a friend who has a loop but she was very sick from it, so my daughter is fearful. She was afraid to get one. She just says, "I hope God will keep me from having children for a while and then I will be operated," that's all.

– What do you think is a good number of children to have in a family these days?

= Maximum three. No more.

ALEXANDRIA

Potted plants, vines, and flowers line the entrance way to a child care center in one of the poorer districts of Alexandria. The large old building also houses a two-room family planning clinic. The organizers hope that women who come to leave their children there will also take advantage of family planning services, or, at least, tell their friends that such services are available.

Several days a week, the director of the Family Planning Association of Alexandria, a remarkably creative woman named Zahia Marzouk, organizes an adult literacy course. She has designed a card game that consists, not of diamonds, hearts and clubs, but of vegetables, fruits, parts of the body, and the word which corresponds to the picture. The Jokers are male-female symbols plus a loop. Playing the game with a teacher, the

players learn about nutrition, about body care, and to read the
names of the objects they see on their cards. Also, through the
Joker, they learn about family planning. There is a great demand
for Zahia's playing cards in Alexandria. [2] Women throughout the
area are now playing with them, teaching each other how to read
and write, and learning the basic skills of hygiene, shopping, and
family planning at the same time.

The woman in the following interview is one of these card
players. Thirty years old and veiled with the traditional black
heik, she has been married twice. Her black eyes looked up at
me only once in a while. She kept her head bowed, and constantly rearranged her veil. Since she had wanted to talk with
us, I could not understand why she showed such signs of being
intimidated, until I realized that it was the presence of Zahia
Marzouk, a local heroine, rather than a visitor from afar, which
awed her.

    – At what age did you marry?
    = I married twice, the first time at 12 years old. Then I got
a divorce, and when I was 24 I got married and had this little
girl.
    – Did you have any children by the first marriage?
    = No, that's why he divorced me. He wasn't any good and
we didn't get children. I asked for the divorce because he
was not a correct person. He used to go around with
women. I didn't like that. It took me some time to get him to
divorce me, but after persistence I succeeded.
    – Had you seen him before you married?
    = No, I was only 12 years old and I didn't know anything
about marriage. I am not from Alexandria originally. I am
from one of the tribes, an Arab tribe. I came to Alexandria
to live with my aunt. There's a lot of difference between my
attitude now and my mother's because mother is an Arab
and she lives in the tribe. I live here and I took over the
habits of Alexandria from my aunt.
    – Tell me about what you call the "different habits?"
    = My mother never sees anybody, never sees a man. She's
too shy to meet a man. I am different because I can meet

[2]An international agency had recently met with Mme. Marzouk to discuss the
possibility of extending the use of her cards to other countries in other lan-
guages.

everybody and go around the market and buy things. But I
am not educated at all. Neither was my mother. I came here
to register for the literacy program.
- How many brothers and sisters do you have?
= I have ten, six sisters and four brothers.
- Did any of them go to school?
= No, because they live in the tribe.
- What happened after your divorce?
= I stayed alone five years, living with my parents. My
second husband is a sailor. I approved this marriage. I saw
him and liked him.
- How many children do you have?
= I have two girls and one boy. The last boy is two months
old. Now I have come here and have had an IUD placed
because I don't want any more children. My husband gave
his permission because he doesn't want any more children
either.
- How did you first hear about family planning?
= I got this letter.

Madame Marzouk interrupted briefly to explain: "When
you have a baby here in Alexandria, you must register with the
Ministry of Health. The Family Planning Association gets the
names and addresses of all couples who have registered new
babies. We send them a nice letter congratulating them about the
newborn child and inviting them to come and visit the family
planning clinic. When she received this letter, she came to see
us. Her husband read her the letter and she came."

- Do you talk with other women about family planning
now that you know about it?
= I am just a new client, but the loop is a very important
thing. Now I want to be a leader. I am going to try to learn to
read and write so I can be a leader and teach other people
about family planning with the cards.
- Did you ever practice a traditional form of birth control
before you knew about modern services?
= I tried *novalgi*. It is like aspirin. Women put it inside the
vagina. It didn't work.
- Why don't you want more children?
= Because of the budget. If I have more children, I won't

be able to keep them properly on the money we have.

— What do you think are the rights of a child? When a child is born, what does he or she deserve in life?

= The child has a right to be fed properly, to be inoculated, to be protected from diseases, and has a right to see a doctor if it is not feeling well.

— And this daughter you're holding must be about six years old. What do you want most for her?

= I want her to be a doctor. I want the child to finish her education before she marries, then I will give her a free choice to pick a husband. If she finishes at 20, if she finishes at 24, it will depend upon her education. I think boys and girls should be educated in the same manner.

— If you could have had an education, what would you have liked to do?

= I would like to be president of an association like this one. I would take care of children as they do here, but I would not like to be in the political field. I don't know how to sew or embroider; I only know housework. But I treat my husband nicely and I try to make him happy. I never thought of asking for more than I have now.

During our series of morning-long discussions at the child care center, one woman questioned us at every occasion, yearning to know more about my visit. Through the interpreter, I asked if she would like to be interviewed. Her face lit up; indeed, she was anxious to talk with me.

At 35, she is married and a trained social worker. Her attitudes are those of many young working women, first-generation working wives who have broken free of traditional roles. Her understanding of the women she serves helped me to perceive the attitudes of women less educated than herself.

= I was married at 22. My father and my husband's father were good friends. The families used to visit each other; that is how we met. We had a three-year courtship, three years of getting to know each other, and then we got married. He works in a district factory as a chemist.

— What about your family and your childhood?

= We have always lived in Alexandria. My mother had 11 children. She could barely read and write. Mother was married when she was 14, and she had no choice in her marriage. The difference between us is that I chose my husband, but only after I graduated from the school of social work and was employed. My father was very important to us. He is educated. He used to teach us at home, and he encouraged us to complete our formal education. The more the children studied, the more he encouraged us.

– How many children do you have?

= Two boys. One is 12 and the other was just 5. My husband is the one who uses family planning because the doctor said it wouldn't be good for me.

– In your duties as a social worker, do you meet many women who resist family planning in any way?

= You know, among the women, nobody resists, or is against, family planning. The men are the people who are sometimes against it. There are many reasons among the various social classes. For instance, even if they are educated, they think that the boy is a very important person in the family because he carries the name of the family. They want children until they get a boy. Sometimes they mistreat the wife for bearing only girls. They don't realize that women have nothing to do with providing the sex of the child. It's a matter of the men's genes. They don't understand; and in the poorer classes they think that, "Well, Allah, the one god, wants it and how could I prevent it?"

– Do you think religious beliefs are a barrier to family planning?

= No, I don't think so. It's the man's own belief when he says, "God." It is not the belief of the religious people.

– Among the women you serve in your work, what do they say is the ideal number of children for a family in these times?

= Minimum two, maximum three. That's what they say.

– What do you think the women here need to improve their situation?

= More nurseries for younger children and babies because if they go to work it would be very hard for them to leave the children, and the labor law gives the mother only half an hour for feeding the child. She does not have the child with her and she has to go home and come back and it's not enough time. So, if she has baby nurseries, she can have a free mind to do her work properly. She will not worry about who is going to feed the child and all.

And women should have truly equal rights with men for the responsibilities of the house, for budgeting, payment, treatment, and caring for the children. The divorce laws, too, are not on the side of women now. A woman has a great deal of trouble in getting her divorce, and sometimes it takes her ten years to go to court and have the right to divorce. Perhaps she won't have any income during that time. Sometimes the law forces the mother to give up her children. The man gets married, and the stepmother treats the children badly.

— Speaking about divorce, do you see many cases of wife beating?

= I've heard about cases. The husband sometimes beats the wife because he wants her money. She's working and he wants to take her money. She refuses and he beats her. He takes it by force. Sometimes he goes out enjoying himself and he comes in drunk or something. He thinks she's not like the woman he was with outside or he wants to see her in a different way so he beats her. It happens even among educated people, but it's less among the educated than among the non-educated. The woman thinks that beating is shameful, that she will expose her family life to others if she complains, so she says nothing. And then, there are those who want to tell everybody about it.

— Speaking for yourself now, what do you consider to be the ideal relationship between husband and wife?

= Oh, there's a lot of differences between the husband and the wife. For the man, the most important thing is the sex relationship. For the woman, it is to have the means to keep the house, care for the children, and have a bit of leisure.

— Do you think the women you know are knowledgeable about sex? Do they have any sex education?

= Our schools do not give girls any idea about sex education, and the parents, even the mothers, think that talking to a girl about such a subject is prohibited. That's why the girl goes off sometimes and loses her way. Even the men don't know much about sexual relations. It comes by experience. Unless he has the experience before he gets married, he knows nothing about it. If he has no experience, both of them will be in the same situation. And then there is the problem of female circumcision.[3] Women cannot be satisfied when they have that. But only the old people are circumcised. Now, because of the law, the younger ones aren't.

— But back to my question, what is the ideal relationship between a husband and a wife?

= A good relationship after marriage: love, and then friendship.

FAYOUM

We passed the pyramids at Giza at 7 in the morning on our way south to the series of oases known as Fayoum. The desert road was almost straight, broken only by a few curves winding around sand dunes. As we neared Fayoum, we could see the soft green color of irrigated land off in a distance. Houses in the oasis villages are built close to the road, and the road wanders from oasis to oasis, in sight of workers in the close-by fields.

We were taken to a village health clinic hidden away in a narrow alley off a marketplace, where I discussed local health problems with a woman doctor who later served as interpreter when we talked with women who were visiting the clinic for a variety of health needs.

The noise of the busy street market outside and the cries of infants cradled in the arms of waiting mothers made it necessary to close both windows and doors in the doctor's small office. The heat of an Egyptian oasis spring settled around us, disturbed only by the buzz of flies that had taken refuge inside with us.

Seated proudly with a child on her knee, a 24-year-old mother waited for our conversation to begin. Preliminary questions revealed that she had been married for seven years and had three children, the oldest seven, the youngest two. She has been planning her family for one-and-a-half years. Her husband is 30 years old and works as a barber in his own small shop. She has never been to school and does not know how to read and write.

— How did you hear about family planning the first time?

---

[3]In its mildest form, the ablation of the clitoris.

= After my last child, I came for a checkup and they told me about family planning. I began to use the loop when the child was just five months old.

– Do you have any side effects or complaints?

= My back hurts sometimes and I am anemic.

– How many children do you want to have?

= After four or five years, one or maybe two more . . . but my husband wants many more.

– How many does your husband want?

= Too many, too many.

– Who delivered your children?

= A doctor.

– Man or woman?

= A female doctor. I would not go to a male doctor.

– What do you want most for your children?

= I want to educate them. I want them to go to the university to be doctors. I want to educate the girls and the boys in the same way. They are the same. I want to educate my sons and daughters and say, "I educated this person, and I educated this one." I will be proud like that.

– Did you ever go to school?

= No, never.

– Do you think your life is different from your mother's?

= Mine is better. My husband has work, and my mother had more children than me, so I am happier than her. I have more money to spend; my house is clean; I have electricity and water.

– Did you know your husband before you married?

= I had met him and liked him, but now . . .

– What do you want to say?

= My husband wants to marry another woman . . . I am anemic, and I am sad because my husband will marry another woman. One woman is enough. I don't understand divorce. That is for God who stands in the heavens. I want to discuss it with my husband but I can't.

– He won't discuss it with you?

= A woman told me that if I discuss it with my husband he will not sleep with me. Some big woman told him he should have a fat wife, so now he is going to look for a fat woman and marry her. Before he had this idea, he was with me, he discussed things with me, he gave all his attention to the

house. After he got it in his mind that he must marry another and more beautiful woman, he began to change his treatment of me. He does not discuss anything with me now. He does not give me the money I need for the house.
— Does he mistreat you?
= He just scolds and quarrels. His voice becomes loud and he says, "I want to beat you!" but he doesn't.
— What would happen if he did beat you?
= I would go to my mother's home and then he would come to take me and say, "I'm sorry," and I would go back with him.
— Was there ever a time when you would rather have been a boy?
= If I had my way, I would be a man because I would have the choice to marry another women, to beat her, to have the last word, yes, that's it, have the last word.

The crowd outside the door of the health clinic was getting more and more noisy. Every now and then I could see a face appear outside the window as some child jumped up to take a look inside. The fan hummed, the children cried, but placidly awaiting our attention was another young woman, 20 years old, the mother of two, aged four and two.

— At what age did you marry?
= Fifteen.
— Are you planning your family?
= I started using the loop two years ago when my youngest was 40 days old. I came here as a pregnant woman, for prenatal care, and heard a lecture on family planning.
— Do you want to have more children?
= I want one more after two or three years.
— Do you have any side effects from the IUD?
= I had some backaches in the beginning, but if I have any complaints I will come here and discuss it with the doctor.
— Did you go to a male or female doctor?

The interpreter leaned forward after speaking with the woman again to say, "She came to me, a woman. She would not have gone to a male doctor."

— Did you ever practice any traditional form of birth control?

= Some women told me about that. They use coffee beans. After their menses, they swallow coffee beans so they won't get pregnant again. I have never done it myself.

— Did you ever go to school?

= No, I don't know how to read and write.

— If you had been able to go to school, what work would you have liked to do?

= I would have been a nurse.

— What do you want most for your children?

= I want to educate them. I want them to go to work as government officials. I don't care if I have boys or girls, but maybe girls are better than boys. The boy doesn't take care of the mother after he gets married, but the girl takes care of her until she is very old.

— How do you spend your day?

= In the morning I prepare a breakfast of beans, then I sweep the floor, I clean the two rooms in the house, then I prepare dinner. Every week I have to bake bread, so sometimes I bake bread, feed the chickens, and that's all.

— Do you work in the fields?

= No. My husband and I sew clothes for the farmers. That is how my husband works, at home. I help him when I have the time.

— Do you see any difference in the way you live and the way your mother lived?

= There is a difference between our lives because my mother had 12 children. She had 12 but only 7 of them are alive now. They died very young. I think my life is better. I lead a good life because I have just two children. I have the time to take care of them, to train them, to take care of the bills, and to take care of a nice home.

IV SUDAN

*"Don't you think this question of family
planning is more of a fashionable idea
with international organizations rather
than a practical help to developing
nations?"* [1]

An official Sudanese government publication quotes the
proverb, "When Allah made the Sudan, Allah laughed".[2] It is
the largest country in Africa, but only one-tenth of its land is
arable. According to the 1973 Census over 17 million people live
in scattered towns and villages, separated from one another by
vast stretches of desert. The 300,000 acres of grazing land barely
support a domestic animal population of 40 million that is growing at the rate of 10 to 15 percent annually, a fact which many
recognize as a serious threat to the nation's agricultural future.
The human population growth rate is estimated to be between
2.8 and 3.3 percent.

A series of officials in Khartoum tried to reassure me saying, "Since the Sudan is such a vast country, it certainly does
not have a population problem. It can hold many more people."

Yet nearly half (45.17 percent) of the Sudanese population
is in the 0–14 age bracket; 73 percent is under 30. Eighty-seven
percent of the total population lives in rural areas that remain,
for the most part, inaccessible to health services and educational facilities. Several doctors with whom I spoke estimated
that over 80 percent of the women they treat are anemic; 87

[1]Question asked author in group discussion at the Sudanese Women's Union,
June 16, 1976, Khartoum.

[2]*Sudan Today,* Ministry of Information and Culture, Khartoum.

44

percent of the children are undernourished. Malaria, tuberculosis, and bilharziasis remain uncontrollable scourges. In the
Southern region, doctors report that "nearly everyone is subject to recurring attacks of malaria." Medical personnel is insuf-
ficient and not increasing fast enough. The Ministry of Social
Welfare estimates that 90 percent of Sudanese women are illiterate, and the Ministry of Education counts 28,826 boys in secondary school nationwide against 8,703 girls. The road system
in the Sudan is desperately inadequate; the government must
rely more and more on jet plane travel for its needs.

Given these bleak statistics, it is not surprising that many
officials say that family planning is not a priority in the Sudan.
Other aspects of population policy take precedence. Dr. Osman
Madawi, chief gynecologist of the hospital in Khartoum, told
me:

"What we have to take into consideration is the health
aspect of the population, mainly. Another aspect is the economic development needs of the country. You see, we have a
wide base in our age structure. We have many young people who
are in need of economic independence, in need of feeding,
upbringing, education, health care, etc. And this need to care for
the population may retard our economic development. That's
the angle on which we are basing our population policy. But
everyone from the high level appreciates that the Sudan needs
more population. Definitely we are aware that we haven't got a
population *problem.*"

Mrs. Mahasin Saad, Secretary-General of the Sudan Family Planning Association, has expressed her views in many
papers.[3] "It is not the size of the population that is important,"
she writes, "but the rate of increase and the age structure of the
population. The rate of increase has its direct bearing on development and a lower rate of population growth is needed to
facilitate the process of development and to raise social and
economic standards for the existing population."

Many with whom I spoke claimed that the government
should do more in the way of informing people, educating them
about health and family planning. Yet the lack of information
sources seemed to be the stumbling block. During a meeting

[3]*The Case for Family Planning in Sudan* and the *Programme of the Sudan
Family Planning Association*, Khartoum, 1975.

with a group of leaders from the Sudanese Women's Union, I heard, "When women know about family planning, they are happy to use it, but so few know about it."

Women blamed superstition, religion and "tradition" for their state. Circumcision of girls was often cited as an example of the low status of women. Yet, when asked whether or not they would, or have already circumcized their daughters, they replied, "Yes."

Women were often reluctant to talk with an outsider. Even highly-educated women in Khartoum sometimes requested that I forego the use of my tape recorder or they made sure that another person was present at our discussion.

PORT SUDAN

The jet flight from Khartoum to Port Sudan takes about one hour. We took off at sunrise; the visibility was perfect. There was nothing to see but mountains of stone, dry earth, sand, and the tiny railway crawling across the desert to the Red Sea. Not until you observe its great dry vastness from an airplane, is it possible to comprehend the difficulties facing the Sudan.

Port Sudan is the supply base of this country. Machinery, supplies, foodstuffs arrive there from abroad and are shipped by train to the capital hundreds of miles away. The town is as parched as the land surrounding it. Goats stroll in the streets. But they are not grazing. There is no grass. The goats are fed straw, then loosed to wander the streets of the city as do the different peoples who inhabit it: Red Sea tribes, black Africans from the south, and northern Sudanese of Arab origin.

In Port Sudan, I met with women of nomadic tribes who have settled in the region and women of the city, young government workers, women in tents on the southern coast; each, I found, led completely different lives. But first, I was taken to Port Sudan's hospital, an imposing building near the center of town. The walls were windowless in the style of colonial hospitals of 40 years ago. People were sitting in the few spots of shade available, waiting for attention or for visiting hours to commence. Here the chief gynecologist was willing to take time away from his patients for a few moments to answer some questions:

– What are the general health problems in this area?
= The main problem is anemia from poor nutrition. In about 80 percent of our cases, the hemoglobin level is below 60. That is why the incidence of abortion is high, premature birth is high. Since yesterday evening we had six cases of spontaneous abortion come to the hospital, and this is mainly due to poor nutrition. They eat mostly meat and milk from the goats. They don't eat fresh food. Vegetables are very expensive.
– What about the circumcision of young girls? Do you see many medical complications from that practice?
= Oh, yes. There are problems of hemorrhage, infection, and retention of urine. I have given lectures on it, but it is still very much practiced. The midwives, the "quack" midwives, perform the circumcision. And if the young girl shows up here, we immediately give anti-tetanus treatment.
– What about complications in childbirth caused by circumcision?
= We have to do a routine anterior episotomy.[4] This is to combat the tightness of the vagina due to the operation.
– And you sew them up again once the child is born?
= Yes, we have to.
– Do many women wish to use family planning?
= Here they are uninterested in it, largely because of ignorance. They don't like the loop. Some of them think the pills are harmful. We have started to give lectures to teach them that there is no harm. But I think if we could get more help on propaganda and more help from the medical staff the situation would improve. An information campaign is the most important factor because, as I say, the women are reluctant. It's not the religious factor or the economic factor. It is just ignorance. We were supposed to start the family planning program here two years ago, but I have yet to receive the materials I need from Khartoum. But, first of all, we have to teach people that this is useful to their lives, only then can we start a good program.

---

[4]In the Sudan, the practice of female circumcision sometimes includes cutting off both sides of the labia minora and majora. The sides are then sewn together, leaving only a small opening for menstrual flow. At childbirth, the woman must be opened by episotomy.

Later on, following a tour of the city and exhausted by the noon-day heat, I had taken refuge in the offices of the Ministry of Social Welfare. The rooms were bare; there was little activity at that time of day, and I was able to talk with several women who work in the Ministry's offices.

A young typist was willing to be interviewed and said I could record the conversation. She had received some formal education and was obviously well-off financially. Her office attire consisted of a European dress covered with the city version of a veil. It is draped over the head and keeps the hands constantly occupied as it must be readjusted each time the wearer moves slightly. Her hands were beautifully manicured. She wore necklaces, bracelets, and rings. She was 21 years old, had attended school for nine years and was planning for her wedding.

    − Do you know your fiancé?

    = I have known him for over a year. We will be married soon.

    − What do you think are the important qualities in a husband?

    = That he speaks to me in a nice manner. He must be an honorable man at home and outside.

    − How many children do you want to have?

    = Two or three. I have talked about this with my fiancé and he agrees. I can get drugs from the midwife.

    − Why just two or three?

    = We already know our economic situation so we must plan for our future. If the economic side gets better than what we now expect, perhaps we will have more, and then if ever there was an accident or something, I would not like to leave many children behind. I don't want to have many children. I can concentrate better on two than on five. And I want my children to be more educated than me.

    − If you had been able to go to school longer, what would you liked to have become?

    = A doctor.

    − Do you think women have as many choices in life as men?

    = They are equal but they have less choices than men.

    − Do you have a radio?

= Yes.
— What kind of programs do you like?
= News and music.
— Have you ever heard of any women leaders on the news programs?
= Just Mrs. Gandhi and Mrs. Thatcher in England. They are leaders.
— If you were to vote for a new president of the country and there was a woman as well-educated as the man running for that office, would you vote for the woman?
= I would not vote for a woman because she would not be as capable as a man.
— But you said you believe men and women are equal.
= Not in all things.

She was becoming agitated. She did not look into my eyes but kept her head bowed, glancing only occasionally at the interpreter for reassurance. Then she protested:

= Your questions are too difficult. I don't think women can be leaders such as men.

The young woman was gradually closing herself off. The interpreter leaned toward me to say, "Women here do not like to mention politics or the laws."

— All right, an easy question. Are you going to continue to work once you are married?
= No.
— Why not?
= My fiancé refused.

ONCE NOMADS

The woman before me wore a threadbare turquoise veil over her head and covering one side of her fine-featured face. In the past years, the nomadic way of life has gradually yielded to fixed settlements around the towns of eastern Sudan. A member of the Beja tribe, nomadic camel-owners of the Red Sea hills, this woman is a resident of a vast wooden camp near Port Sudan. Many men of the tribe, including her husband, have gone elsewhere to work as paid laborers, leaving behind the women and an occasional male family member.

Her house consisted of two small rooms and a courtyard used both as bedroom and kitchen. Each house in the settlement has its own water tap but no electricity. Drinking cups were made from tin cans; the only dishes visible were large earthen cooking pots. We sat in the courtyard on wood-and-rope cots. The sun was setting, and as we talked, one by one, the women got up and went to a corner of the courtyard to say the evening prayer. All of them wore gold rings in one side of their noses and each had a different colored veil, faded by frequent washings.

Wide-eyed children watched us closely. A little boy of about three seemed to be favored, since he was the only child whose total nakedness was decorated with a necklace of beads.

When the interpreter explained to the women that I would like to talk with them, they agreed but remained suspicious and refused to let me tape our conversation. I took notes in the darkness as night fell around us. Later, the interpreter explained that these cautious women fear cameras, government cars, and husbands. They run and hide in the courtyards when the social worker comes on a regular visit.

The woman whose house it was seemed more apathetic than cautious. She thinks she is about 30 years old, but because she is thin and frail looks 20 years older. She has two living children; two others died at birth. She explained that she had a fever just before childbirth so the children were born dead.

— How many people live here with you?
= A son of 18, a daughter of 15. My son mends rope at the port. My three brothers and their wives live here too, as well as all these children you see.
— What kind of food do you find to eat here?
= We grind beans to make flour, then cook it with water. It makes a sort of porridge. We serve it with milk. We have butter from goat's milk and a few dates. That's all. It is like that every day.
— Have there been any health problems in the family?
= No. No disease, just general fatigue all the time. We have no sugar to put in our coffee.

She went on to speak of her life:

= My mother died when I was a small child. I never went to school and was married as soon as I reached puberty. My daughter, now 15, went to school until she was 11, but she failed her tests and lost interest. She refuses to go anywhere now, to a training class or anything, because she is shameful of her failure. Her father doesn't care. He is not interested in education.

− What do *you* think about education?

= It is good, but not to work outside. I don't think women should leave the house.

Following a few more questions, I asked her if she thought men had more advantages in life than women. She came back to the question of work and, to a certain degree, contradicted her former reply.

= I would prefer to have been a boy, to be able to work outside. Girls are only for marriage.

− Have you ever heard of any traditional method of limiting the size of a family or limiting the number of births in a family?

She lowered her eyes and I could feel that she resented my question.

= Never! That is a sin.

HUSHERI, A SCHOOL

The Red Sea was about a mile off to our left as we drove south toward Suakin, the ancient port of Sudan. We could see ships far out to sea; their images shimmered through the heat of the sand between us. From time to time, huts of sticks and straw matting, with goats or camels tethered nearby, broke the monotony of the desert scene. Each house was far from the next. Even settled, the nomadic people try to preserve their privacy as strictly as before. Only the ubiquitous dust crosses the threshhold of their homes.

Nearly an hour passed before the truck pulled off the road and drove toward three wooden cabins standing on a dune amidst wiry shrubs. These buildings are the primary school that serves a huge area to the South and West whose people are partially settled. They grow watermelons and tomatoes, but they continue to migrate with goats and camels during the dry months.

There were 39 students in all: 32 boys, 7 girls. Most were barefoot. Floury dust covered them and everything else: school building, benches, books, and soon ourselves. Everything in the school was handmade: tables, benches, geography maps, and natural science diagrams. One of the three buildings serves as a dormitory. Boys, whose families live too far or have gone off herding elsewhere, may stay here under the supervision of the schoolmaster.

We were told we could visit some women if we did not take any pictures or use the recorder and were escorted over the sand to a lean-to built on the summit of a high dune. Several yards to the left was a house made of sticks and straw matting. Its door was a ragged piece of burlap.

We sat in the shade of the lean-to's palm leaf roof and talked with a widow who guessed that she was about 40 years old. She was veiled in dark blue and held the ragged material across her face, just under the nose. She wore a gold ring in one nostril; it seemed to accentuate the delicate, slender features common to this desert tribe.

The schoolmaster served as interpreter to my interpreter, for the local tribal language was not known to her. The woman has three living children; three died when they were young. The eldest is 15; the youngest 9. They eat mostly ground bean flour as do the great majority of the people of this region.

She apologized several times for having nothing to offer me, saying, "You understand, we don't have much." While the schoolmaster explained the object of my visit, a child appeared with a tin can filled with water. We drank gratefully. Later, when I learned how far this woman must go to fetch water, and the process she had to go through to remove its salt content, I realized how precious her "nothing" was.

First, I asked her how far away was the nearest doctor?

= I have to go to Port Sudan about 40 miles to the north. But my family is rarely sick. It's only me. I am always tired.
− How have you taken care of your family since your husband died?

= I work in the school, cleaning it. This way I get a bit of money. I like work but I want to earn more.

− Do your children go to school?

= Yes, but the daughter only went four years. I took her out so she could help at home. Since I work in the school, my daughter must stay home and cook.

− If your daughter had finished her education, would you permit her to work?

= Yes, but I don't know what work, for there is no work in this part of the country. I want my son to learn to speak Arabic so he can become an official in the government.

− Can you tell me how your life differs from that of your mother?

= My mother had a more restful life. She had more money. I am very poor since my husband died, but even before that, my life was worse than hers. I have no skills. I don't know how to do anything. If I knew how to sew I could make things for other people and earn a bit of money.

− What do you think the women of this area need most?

= A clinic for health. We should have a qualified midwife and a water supply. We have to walk about a mile to get our water and it is not good. It is too salty. We have to distill it ourselves and it takes much time.

− At what age do you want your daughter to marry?

= When someone comes to ask for her.

− How many children do you think your daughter should have?

= As many as come. It is up to God.

− What do you want people to say about you when you are old?

= That I was a religious woman who always said her prayers and who did her best to raise her family and to help other people.

WAD MEDANI

The Gizira scheme is the pride of Sudanese agriculture. Five million acres of clay plains between the White and Blue Niles have expanded both food production and the national cash crop, cotton. We had driven out into the Gizira from Khartoum to attend ceremonies in several villages of the area. In each town a crowd awaited the visiting Minister, men to one side of the road, women and children to the other. Speeches, ribbon-cutting, and a noisy departure of the official fleet of cars was the usual scene.

After two such visits, we stopped to rest in a government guest house. Three unmarried women, an older grandmother, and I began talking as we waited for the journey to continue. At one point the discussion turned to the practice of the circumcision of little girls. Each of the women said she had been circumcised as a child. They had had the clitoris excised and three of them had been subjected to more extensive surgery. Each woman wanted to tell me the story of her circumcision. One, a 25-year old student's was typical.

= My mother didn't want me to have the operation, but my grandmother took me and had it done. I was just eight years old. There is a special woman who does this, a sort of midwife. She does it in her house. It took five people to hold me down.

The neighbors and the family come. It is like a ceremony. They attend the operation and want to watch. There is no anaesthetic and people keep saying, "Cut a bit more here, cut a bit more there." Then they sew it together again. They take you to the Nile at sunset for a ceremony. Sometimes you can't urinate for five or six days or longer, it hurts so. When you get married, it might take a month or two weeks for the man to penetrate. There is much trouble with this. It is a primitive practice, and it's stupid, after all.

— And why do you think this practice is kept alive?

= It is not so much a question of virginity any more, but it is for the pleasure of the man. He enjoys it, and after one or two years he will help you to go and rearrange yourself, have it sewn again so that you are tight for him.

— You say you are engaged to be married. How many children do you want to have?

= I am going to be married in a month. I want four children. I think four is enough. Nowadays life is expensive. You have to work so hard.

— What about your daughters and circumcision?

= Well, it depends on their father. If he likes it, I will do it, if not, I won't. Also my mother has her opinion. All the family has its say. If I don't do it, my mother will ask, "Why don't you want to do it?" It is almost compulsory.

Questions about the different methods of family planning took over the conversation. The young woman wanted to know about each method. She said that she had heard, "the tablets have something bad. Sometimes you find yourself miserable." Each woman mentioned a rumor she had heard about family planning methods. But I returned to the first young woman to ask her more about herself.

    — What are you studying?
    = Law, because women are working in politics now. I think it is better for us to study more. I will marry in another month. It will be difficult for me but I will do my best to study because my husband has finished the university. I want to keep up with him.
    — Does he want you to continue your studies after marriage?
    = Well, he didn't refuse. When I talked to him, he didn't refuse it—but I don't know what will happen after we marry.

JUBA

The Southern provinces of the Sudan are bordered by the Central African Republic, Zaire, Uganda, Kenya, and Ethiopia. The southern region is separated from the north by an impenetrable area known as the Sudd swamp. Together the provinces count a population of 3 million people of 31 different tribes. The south was attached to the Islamic north in the 19th century under the British administration, but in recent years conflicts between the Muslim north and the animist and Christian south greatly hindered the development of the southern portion of the Sudan until 1973 when the southern provinces were granted regional autonomy. The flights of the Sudan Airways jets are Juba's only regular communication link to the north and to the outside world.

The bulk of health services in the south are delivered by medical assistants. At present there is one midwife for every

18,251 people.[5] I was to learn that over 90 percent of the population in the south suffers from malaria and 97 percent of the women are anemic.

While in Juba, I met a woman member of the regional Parliament. I interviewed her in the hospital where her three-month old daughter was critically ill with malaria. She was a handsome woman of 29, tall, as are the people of the Dinka tribe, wearing a yellow European dress, free of veils or decoration. Her eyes were direct and proud.

– Were you born here in Juba?
= No, I'm from Umbek. I went to primary school there, then to a mission school in Khartoum and to Khartoum University. I studied economics and political science.
– Tell me about your family.
= My father was the chief of one of the tribes. They tend to have a lot of wives. My father had many. I think he had about 20 children in all, considering that many died as well. I am the only well-educated woman in the family. I guess it was out of sheer luck. I happened to be one of those who was sent to school. My father wanted it, not my mother. She was very much opposed to my education in the early stages. She wanted me to relieve her of the family work at home, so she was very upset. I was the only one who did well in school so my father developed interest. Seeing that I was promising in my studies, he kept encouraging me until I got my highest education.
– How many children do you have?
= I was married four years ago. I have three children. It is very tiring to have them so rapidly, but I thought it would be better to have children at the beginning so that later on I can do other things. If I have to give birth all my life, I don't think I'll be able to do anything else. I thought it's better to finish with children now, and then afterwards, I will have time for other things.
– What kind of work do you do here?
= I'm in Parliament and I sometimes participate in women's activities. I'm secretary of the Women's group of the

[5]*Primary Health Care Program, Southern Region Sudan, February, 1976—Juba.* The Democratic Republic of the Sudan.

Sudan Council of Churches. This group was formed essentially to help women in things like nutrition, education, child care, how to maintain a house—all the things that women need in their lives. Also, we want to help them become self-reliant in sewing and handicrafts so that instead of buying from the market they can make things and sell them as a source of income.

— What do you feel are the primary needs of women here in the south?

= The primary need is health care. You have seen this hospital. You have seen that most of the patients are women and children. They are not healthy. They need a better diet. You find that the food eaten in most homes lacks vitamins, calcium, and iron. Women do not know where they can get vitamins or the type of food that should be given to a child who is young. You find children eating the same food as adults. So nutrition education, teaching women the requirements of the body, that is necessary. They need enlightenment on these things.

And they need enlightenment to help themselves to become economically independent because the bulk of Southern women are not educated. Sometimes they have no husband to care for them. They can do no work; they cannot even think of how to help themselves. If women had some basic education, they would be able to find some work. Crafts is one thing, for example, but we need markets for crafts. And farming—traditional farming at present is not all that useful. You find women just clearing a small area around their home to try to get a few things like ground nuts and vegetables, but if they can start to expand so that there is enough for the family to eat as well as a surplus, then it could be taken to the market.

— Is legal and political awareness part of your activities in the Women's Group?

= Yes, indeed. Our Constitution grants women equal rights in all walks of life, equal pay, equal job opportunity and so on, but there are times when people exploit the ignorance of our women. Not many of our women know what is in the Constitution because not many of them are educated. Even those who are educated do not know the importance of what is in the Constitution. We also have the basic principles of the Sudanese Socialist Union. It has given freedom to women to participate with men in every aspect of life, but, for example, where this right has been infringed, women don't know how to fight for it. They don't know their rights.

An example I might give is the right of a woman to be employed in a government department. Sometimes the man responsible might want to use that position as a favor to a certain woman he wants to—you know—to make the woman feel that this was not given to her because it is her right, but given to her because this man made it possible. She must owe him something, then he can exploit her and play games with her. You find women in low-level jobs are bullied by their bosses because they don't know their rights.

The bulk of women don't know what is happening. They just hear things. They are cut off from information. It is up to us educated women to help them. This is the major job for us. This is what I hope to be able to do.

YOUNG TRAINEES

Seventeen young women of four different tribes were sitting primly in a row one Sunday morning at Juba Hospital, hands folded on their knees. They were dressed in white uniforms and sandals, waiting to meet the visitor. These young women are students at the school for midwives. Each had been selected by the chief of her tribe to come to Juba town to learn how to conduct normal deliveries, to learn the elements of hygiene, nutrition, and infant feeding.

Few among these women had ever been to school. They come from families who live partially naked in the bush country of Southern Sudan. Here they will train for two years and then return to their tribes. Under this program, they will not be allowed to work elsewhere but in their own village.

In their home area 90 percent of the children are anemic from malaria, hookworm, or poor nutrition. The chief gynecologist told me most of the women he treats have a hemoglobin level of 30 percent. Infertility due to syphillis and tuberculosis is a major medical problem in the South. Sending these

young midwives back into the countryside is viewed as only a
start in solving the health problems of the area. Given the high
infant mortality rate of the region, there are no family planning
programs.

Among the students with whom I spoke was a divorcee of
26. She was 18 when she married, is a member of the Zande
tribe, and is a Catholic.

- Do you have any children?
= No.
- Did you want to get divorced?
= Yes, my husband was beating me, mistreating me. You
know, sometimes if the husband has another wife he will
mistreat you.
- Did your husband have other wives?
= Yes, there were two, but that was not so bad. It was just
the husband who was not a good man.
- Does your father have more than one wife?
= No, only one.
- How many brothers and sisters do you have?
= Four brothers and two sisters. The eldest brother went
to school until he finished technical school. The other
brothers and sisters did not go to school at all.
- If you married again someday, what qualities do you
want to find in a husband?
= I want my husband to be kind and a hard worker. I want
him to look after the family at home.
- And how many children would you like to have?
= Four.
- How are you going to keep from having more?
= I will become too old.

I asked the interpreter to question her to find out if she
knew about modern family planning methods.

After some discussion between the two, the interpreter
looked up and said, "She has heard of the pill but she doesn't
know how it works."

- Would you educate your daughters as much as your
sons?
= I would help the girls more because when they grow up

the girls will be the only ones looking after me. My brother did not care for my mother, that's why I want girls. At least they will look after me just as I do for my mother. I wanted to become a midwife because my father and mother are old. My brothers and sisters had not been to school. They are only digging in the gardens. I thought it would be good to become a midwife so I could help my parents. I met some girls who had taken this course. I saw that they learned good things, that if someone becomes a midwife, it will help the country. That's why I have chosen it. Now I can help my country.

– Tell me, have you seen any changes in your life as compared with your mother's life?

= The difference is that I have become cleaner than she is. I used to work hard digging in the ground, doing everything in the house, cleaning and digging. I would get all dirty. I didn't know about hygiene or how to clean myself. Now I know.

– Do you want to teach other women about hygiene when you go back to your tribe?

= Yes, I will teach them. They have enough water but they have no knowledge.

– What do you think the women of your tribe need most to learn?

= Women want to learn the new things in health and learn how to dig and work hard in their gardens and in the house. A housewife should learn about cooking and cook different things. I will try my best to teach them.

– Was there ever a time in your life when you thought it would be better to have been a boy?

= I thought of it when I was quite old. I thought the life of a boy was better. His education is better than a girl's. I knew I could be of more help to my parents if I were a man.

– But if boys and girls have the same education, do you see any difference between them?

= No, none.

– If you had been able to go to school, what work would you have liked to do?

= A teacher.

– Not a midwife?

= No, teacher.

— And what do you want most for your children?
= I want to feed them, to give them all the food they need. I
want them to have clothes. I want them to be clean.
— One last question. When you get married again, what
would happen if your husband told you he didn't want you
to work?

The young woman laughed aloud. The interpreter began to
laugh also, then turned to say, "If her husband won't let her
work, she says, she will divorce him."

V SRI LANKA

*"We must give women confidence. One of
the major problems is that women feel
they are inferior, that 'our brains are not
so educated.' Timidity is a problem, fear
of speaking up . . ."*

Kumari Jayawardene[1]

On the road signs the graceful, curving Sinhalese script was
being replaced by English lettering. The small island nation of
Sri Lanka was preparing for a big event. In just two weeks,
delegations from the world over would be arriving for the
Non-Aligned Summit Conference. The capital city was bustling
with preparations. Streets were being cleaned, buildings re-
painted, an entire highway rebuilt. Even the lush vegetation of
Colombo—trees, plants, vines—was being cut and trimmed.
Everywhere people were at work to ensure the visitors would be
properly welcomed.

   Sri Lanka is one of the most densely populated countries of
the world. With 14 million inhabitants, the population density is
514 persons per square mile. Seventy-five percent of the population lives in rural areas.

   Yet Sri Lanka has some unusual features for a developing
nation. Its citizens have benefited from free universal education
since 1945. The literacy rates are 85 percent for men, 71 percent
for women. Twenty-six percent of the total work force is female.
Fifty-five percent of all children are born in medical facilities.
There is one doctor for every 5,000 inhabitants. In addition, the
island has a remarkable transportation system: 11,000 buses

[1]Political scientist, interviewed July 14, 1976, Colombo.

move over one-fourth of the population each day.

Another set of figures reminds us, however, that Sri Lanka is troubled by problems common to other developing nations. In 1974, it was found that 14 percent of pre-school children suffered from third-degree protein calorie malnutrition; 1 million children are said to be victims of various degrees of PCM. Unemployment and limited economic opportunity for the well-educated populace is another of the country's urgent problems. Unemployment on the island stands at 14 percent of the work force, or nearly 1 million people. Each year hundreds of university graduates leave the island in search of better paid employment elsewhere. Sri Lanka ranks high on the list of nations affected by the brain drain.

Women suffer from the employment problem as much as men. Dorothy Abeywickreme, president of the Association of University Women, told me that her organization had just received a grant enabling it to teach typing to 8,000 women university graduates, "that they might become employable."

Women are the majority in most university faculties. In 1976, 50 percent of the enrollment of the medical faculty was female. This is not viewed with satisfaction by some, and consideration is now being given to limiting the number of women students in medical studies.

The women of Sri Lanka are far better educated than women of other Asian countries, yet the superstitions, taboos, and customs passed along from ancient feudal times continue to persist regardless of ethnic or religious origin. In conversations with educated women in Colombo, I was told about superstitious beliefs that still deprive rural women of self-confidence and autonomy.

Higher education levels, unemployment, and the dowry system were reasons offered for the rise in marriage age among the Sri Lankans, and thus the decline in the population's growth rate of recent years. Unemployed young men cannot marry; they must wait to find a job. Girls who seek higher education, then employment, put off marrying until both are achieved; and the families of young girls have difficulty raising the money for dowries. The less educated the girl, the more the parents must provide for her dowry: the husband must be compensated for her ignorance.

WENNAPPUWA

Wennappuwa is a village 60 miles north of Colombo along the coastal route. A Land-Rover, minus its shock absorbers, took us there early one morning. Once off the main road, we drove past palm groves, banana trees, and small gardens to stop at a schoolhouse. It was nestled among tall trees and surrounded by flowering plants of an amazing diversity. Benches were placed in the large central room. To the left was a tiny, book-filled office where the private conversations took place later in the morning. Our host was a young Singhalese Catholic priest. He quickly sent children scattering to collect women of the village to talk with us. While we awaited their arrival, the tiny school children sang for us and showed us their work.

We were told that the older women were busy with their chores, but that several younger women were free and willing to talk with us. These young girls were typical of the new generation of rural women who are educated but languish without employment in rural areas. The first was 28 years old, unmarried, and dressed in a European skirt and blouse. Her long dark hair was worn in a single braid, drawn to one side over her left shoulder. She had attended school until the age of 16. She had wanted to talk with us, but seemed desperately nervous all the same.

— Do you think your life is any different from your mother's or your grandmother's life?
= I don't know much about my grandmother but my mother certainly does not have the independence that I have now. I am very fortunate to be able to go to meetings and work in the women's committee. My mother was tied to the house. Her life was dominated by her father and mother. My mother had no say in her life, but I have independence.
— What do you mean by "independence?"
= While I was growing up, my father was away from here. He was working in a fishing business in another village. I had to pay heed to my elder brother for all things. When I was in the upper school, he didn't allow me to visit a friend or go about on my own. I was not allowed out after six o'clock. That is over now; I come and go as I please. You

see, after six o'clock girls are not allowed out because the evil spirits, the black prince, will follow them and, it is widely believed, tempt them. These are the beliefs of the rural people. Now I am very independent in this village, in my group. I can go about because of my work with the women's organizations.

– What do you think the women of this village need most?

= A lot of people are still dominated by their parents. I see that, now that I have gained my freedom. The parents of the younger girls must be instructed that if the girls are given the freedom to come out, join committees and work together, they will be better off, better off in the sense that they will learn more things. They want more freedom; they must not be dominated. It's just like trees growing in the shade. We cannot be "trees growing in the shade."

– You say you are not married, but tell me, what are the qualities you seek in a husband?

= My married friends, after a certain time, always complain and say they are not happy in their marriages. The couple doesn't enjoy the marriage; they don't get along together. Some marriages are made because the parents force them to marry. Some women, when they have a certain number of children, think they should have no more. The woman will say "enough," but the man doesn't care. He is not concerned about it—he will just have as many as come—it is not *his* problem. The man wants sex, and the children come. After a certain period, the woman doesn't want to have relations for fear of more children. Then the man has sex outside.

– But isn't there another way of avoiding having children besides refusing the man?

= You mean not having children but having relations? I have heard that there are ways to prevent births so that you can still live in harmony with your man. Yet the women in this area, they are afraid. They say it is harmful. They say there are after-effects, that you won't live long after you start using these things. Those are the married ones; they are saying they are afraid to take contraceptives. They think it will have effects on our health. I heard a lecture about this once but when it was over the women said they wouldn't accept.

– Once you marry, do you know how many children you would like to have?

= I am more worried about my husband—what sort of man he will be. That is more important than the number of children I will have. I am not really that keen on getting married. I worry a lot about the kind of man I will get.

– Why so much worry? Are you afraid? Do men beat their wives or what?

= Yes, the fishermen along the coast beat their wives. But it is usually because they have fights over money, earnings; both parties are at fault.

– What do you want to do with your life since you are not so keen on getting married?

= I want to be a group leader. I want to get women together for work purposes. If I can help them, I will get much satisfaction.

The next young woman who talked with us was older. She told us she was celebrating her birthday that very day. Her hair was cut short. She, too, wore a European dress. She was much less nervous, more mature and poised, than the woman before her.

– So you are 31 years old today. Congratulations! Tell me about your family, brothers and sisters. Are you married?

= I am not married, just engaged. My father married twice; I am from the second marriage, four children from the first and then two with my mother. My father died when I was six so mother looked after all the children and raised us alone. She was a fisherwoman—catching, drying, and selling fish.

– Do you mean she cast the nets herself?

= Yes, on the beach, then she sold the fish and a few vegetables. Now most of the children have gone. Only my mother and I remain at home. My brother gives a bit of money from time to time. My godparents took him and educated him. We are all Catholics.

– How long did you go to school?

= Through secondary school. I couldn't sit for the exams because I became ill. I applied for various jobs but couldn't find work. Then the women's organization was started in this village. I joined in the hope of better prospects for a job. When you are a member of the Mahila Samithi[2] you can get a letter to support you when you apply for a job. But after that I didn't really need a job because I became so interested in social work, and we had started a canteen, so I got enough money from that. We prepare food and sell it. We are a group, a cooperative. We share the tasks and the earnings. We get 2 rupees a day and 25 rupees each at the end of the month.

— Can you tell me what you feel is the important difference between your life and your mother's?

= We had a very hard time before. My mother had to bring up all the younger brothers and sisters. Even after marriage, she had a lot of problems. Compared to my mother, my life is 100 percent better. Sometimes we had no food, sometimes no clothing at all. But now we have family comforts. It is true for most of the village. Most of the younger generation is better off than their parents were at the same age.

— What do you think is the biggest change here in this village?

= Well, the area has prospered. Social change has taken place since my mother's time. The village prospered because of the women's organization and small cottage-industries and such developments. Now the girls do not idle at home. They work rolling cigarettes, making brooms, and handicrafts. They have small industries like that. Some do tailoring. In my mother's time there was no such thing.

— And what do you think are the principal needs of the women here?

= Some, they just like to idle at home—they don't come forward and get themselves involved in any work. They are very backward. That is why some people are suffering. What we should do is go to the homes of these backward people and ask them to come and see the work that has been done and make them, somehow, participate in the activities and try to show them a better way of life.

A young girl about 7 years old opened the door of the office

---

[2]A national women's organization.

where we sat and politely directed a question to the young woman before me. In a patient tone the question was answered. The child smiled and the door closed once again. Later I was to learn that the question had been about the cookies and soft drinks being prepared for us outside. I continued, asking:

    – Tell me what qualities you seek in a husband.

    = I want him to be a good person who will be interested in the family, who won't drink, and who won't waste the money, whatever little we have. I don't mind if a person does not have a big salary or a big job, but he must be employed in a small way because with my small earnings we can pool our money, even if it is little. What I want is peace in the family and that he be a good person. I am engaged to be married already, you know.

    – How did you meet your fiancé?

    = He has no mother, no family. He has to prepare his meals and take them to his workplace. One of my friend's mother arranged it, thinking that he needed to be married. I have met him but I have not spoken. In groups, yes, but not alone. He hasn't come to my mother officially, but I think he is coming soon. I have asked several people; they say he doesn't take liquor. I think I like him very much.

    – Do you have any idea how many children you would like to have, once married?

    = Three or four.

    – Why not more?

    = If we have enough money, it doesn't matter having more children. My fiancé has a steady income but we do not have property. We have nothing to back us. We have only our daily wages. That is all we can earn. If we were very well off, we would have lots of property, we could afford more children. But with the present situation, we can't have more than three or four because the children would have to suffer. I want to educate them well. I want them to have good jobs. I want to look after them well and see that they are provided for. We would have too little time to give them attention and love if there were many more.

    – But it is normal for a woman to have many more. How are you going to avoid more births?

    = On my own I won't be able to decide that, how to have a

few. On my own, I may not be able to solve that problem. I have only the idea that I don't want more—but I don't know how.

THE HIGHLANDS, A TEA PLANTATION

The most noticeable feature of a car trip into the highlands of Sri Lanka is the lack of open spaces. Everywhere the eye looks, there are houses or people or animals: evidence of human settlement. The lush green rice paddies are veined with walkways going from one habitation to another. Another village is around every turn in the road. Its streets are filled with merchants, markets; people are everywhere, and they seem little bothered by the billows of black smoke that engulf them as buses, trucks, vehicles of all sorts, belch through the towns.

As we climbed higher, the vegetation changed suddenly. The rounded mountains of the tea plantations have been denuded of their trees and are covered with what at first appears to be soft green moss. Observed more closely the tea bushes are not gracious plants; they stand chest high and have strong, sharp branches. Among them move in colored saris the women "pluckers," with 80-pound baskets strapped around their foreheads and onto their backs. Impatiently they throw the tea leaves over their shoulders into the baskets to the tune of a foreman's constant chastisement: "Pluck here, pluck there, quickly, quickly!"

These women work from early morning to late afternoon for the sum of 4.70 rupees a day, roughly 45 U.S. cents. They do so whether it be hot, cold, or rainy. They work quickly and silently, covered when the rains come with a piece of plastic sheeting. Their bare feet grip the roots of the bushes to maintain balance on the steep mountainside. As we wound up the mountain to the first plantation, women enroute to the factory moved to one side as the car passed. They turned to look, and smiled—without the slightest hint of the shyness of which I had been warned.

The quarters of the plantation workers were down a steep hill and formed a series of long bungalows. Four families live in one. Each lodging consists of a kitchen, an entrance way, and one medium-sized room. There is no water inside, no electricity. The courtyard was well swept and, at this mid-afternoon hour, filled with older people—too old to work in the fields. Some small children, raggedly dressed and barefoot, were doing their best to crawl away from the watchful eyes of the grandmothers. It was cold and damp. We became chilled quickly as we waited for the pluckers to return.

The woman with whom we talked was 45 years old, a Hindu. She had changed from her "work sari" into attire suitable for visitors: a sari of worn mauve cloth. Her teeth were reddened by betel leaves, chewed during the work day, and rotting; two were missing. She looked undernourished. Speaking in a soft, submissive tone, she told us she had carried nine children. The last, a girl, had died just over a year ago. The youngest is three, the eldest 20. She has always lived on this plantation and never attended school. She started plucking tea when only 10 years old.

> — How old were you when you had your first child?
> = I attained puberty when I was 12, so I was married at 12. My parents arranged the marriage. I did not know my husband before. I was 13 when my first baby came.
> — Can you tell me how you think your life is different from your mother's or your grandmother's life?
> = My mother had just three children. I have a younger sister and an elder brother. As a child I was all right, but now I find it extremely difficult to live because I have such a large family—eight children. That's the main difference.
> — What do you think is a good family size in today's times? What is the best number of children per family?
> = If people have more than three, they will find it extremely difficult to make out.
> — And what are you telling your daughters about having smaller families?
> = I won't say anything to them. I am a poor example, myself. And then, having a child is so good.
> — Do you know of any methods of limiting the number of children in the family?
> = I know some women who were about three months pregnant. They went out somewhere and got some kind of medicine. They bought it, but it didn't work. I don't know what it was.

- Was it an herb or did they get it from a pharmacy?
= I don't know. Then there was another woman who was not married, but she became pregnant. She was a widow. She had a daughter and was living with her parents. It was during that time that she had come to know some man. She thought her pregnancy would be a shame and a slur on her family. She tried to abort by using some kind of medicine but it didn't work. Later she drank some insecticide to commit suicide.
- But you don't know of any modern methods which work?
= No, I don't.
- Can you tell me what you think the women here on this plantation need most? What would make their lives better?
= You know, we are a bit scared. For any improvement of our life on the estate, we have to ask the superintendent. Normally, we all have large families, and we have only these "line" rooms, with hardly any space on the small veranda. There are too many people. The one room is not enough. We have gone to the superintendent and asked him for another room. Perhaps the problem would be solved if we were a smaller family. We need more money. If only we could just go to the superintendent and ask for loans. And then there is hygiene. We have tap water for everyone but it is far, 300 yards away. We need a better water supply and more lavatories.
- And now a silly question. Did you ever think that it might have been better to have been born a boy?
= Oh yes, I have thought of it several times. If I had been born a male I wouldn't have to go through all this agony of bearing so many children and have all these difficult problems to face. I think if I were a man I wouldn't have as many problems.

Despite the late hour, another tea plucker was willing to talk with us. She sat before us, dressed in a faded yellow sari, nursing a year-and-a-half-old baby, well wrapped up for warmth. The child had on woolen socks and a cotton cap, below which its eyes were dull, almost dead-looking. The mother wore gold pins in each nostril and gold earrings on each ear. She had a bright red caste spot in the center of her forehead. Slowly, she told us she had never attended school and did not know her husband before marriage.

— Tell me about your mother's life? How do you think yours is different?
= My mother had ten children. I have five brothers and four sisters. But although we were many, things were all right then. The situation is different now. Even though I have only three children, life is too costly.
    My husband and I both work on the plantation 30 days a month. I am a very good plucker, but with all the deductions for rations, we might get something like 150 rupees ($14 US) at the end of the month.
— Were your parents also tea pluckers?
= Yes, but in those days the wages sufficed. Now I am able to save about 25 rupees ($3 US) a month. I have a bit saved and am trying to get some jewelry for the children.
— So the only difference you see from your mother's time is the cost of living?
= Yes, that is it.
— Do you want more children?
= No, I don't want any more, and I have already had a tubectomy. I had it done after this baby was born. This one is a boy and I have two girls.
— When you and your husband discussed the operation, why was tubectomy chosen rather than vasectomy?
= My husband was a bit afraid, for one thing. I didn't want to have any more babies to add more burdens to my life and his, and at the time I didn't know there was such a thing as vasectomy that males can do. I didn't know it.
— How did you manage to work and pluck tea all day when you were pregnant?
= There is no leave for pregnancy. I go to work around 7 o'clock and work until lunchtime at 12:30. Then at 1:30 we start picking again. It is too little time to go home, and we finish work at half-past four. Then we have to weigh in the baskets. No leave is given.
— Did you go to the hospital to have your babies?
= I had them in the lines (while picking tea) and then, this last one, I didn't go to work for thirteen days. After I went

to the hospital to undergo tubectomy I didn't work for three months.
  − Did you feel you needed three months' rest?
  = I felt a little weak and there was no one to care for the baby. Now there is a woman to look after the child when I go to the fields. I just come back to breastfeed the child, if I can, then I go to pick again.
  − Do other women you know talk openly about family planning?
  = Many women have asked me, since the operation, if there are any side effects or problems. We used to discuss it quite openly, as well as in secret. There is one woman on the estate who has had a child every year. She has seven children already. I told her she should do the same thing I did, and six months ago she listened to my advice and had a tubectomy.
  − How did you first hear about family planning?
  = My brother has three children, and his wife can't nurse her babies. They had to buy milk for them. My brother found it too expensive to bring up those babies so he took his wife to the hospital and made her undergo the operation. She has a son and two daughters, and they are fine; so I thought, "Why not me? This way we can live more happily."
  − What do you want most for your children?
  = I just wish that they wouldn't have to do this plucking. I hope they can at least get some sort of education, maybe a chance of getting some kind of decent employment.
  − Among the women you know who work here on the plantation, what do you think they need most in order to improve their lives?
  = The people here are totally ignorant of everything. I would like somebody to teach us child care and how to behave nicely with people. They are a nasty lot. I was the first woman to undergo tubectomy, and all those people have been scolding and teasing me saying, "Why did you ever do that?" That's the type of people you get in these estates. Somebody should come here and instruct them and advise them on the *benefits* of family planning and of limiting their families.
  For me, I thought, since I have three children, that's

enough, so why have more and then get into a mess of troubles. I will try to give the children, at least, the best: food, clothing, good health . . .

MASKELIYA HOSPITAL

Perched on a mountainside at 4,500 feet altitude, Maskeliya Hospital dominates hills and valleys below. We had gone to the hospital one morning to listen to a lecture given by visiting workers from the Family Planning Association of Sri Lanka. The hospital was large and airy, the corridors wide and empty. As we sat in the second floor lecture room, listening to the presentation, a dog kept walking up and down the corridor, snuffling about for a missing master.

The Family Planning team introduced me to a group of 20 men and women. The women sat on the benches facing us, the men stood to one side. Listening to the speaker, the women appeared to be far more at ease than their menfolk. The men had the look of well-disciplined workers: empty, tired, and frightened. The women had a more conspiratorial attitude. Soon we were talking about my visit and asking for volunteers for personal interviews.

Alone in a vast lecture room, we sat with a woman whose sari was covered with a terrycloth bathrobe cut off at the waist to serve as a coat here in the mountain clime. She wore the gold filigree earrings common here. Thirty-nine years old and a Buddhist, she said she had never worked; she is a housewife.

— What does your husband do?
= We don't have any land. He runs errands and does work for a hotel. We have eight mouths to feed on just one man's earnings. It's difficult. I have six children; the youngest is three. The eldest daughters got through the tenth grade, and I have a son who is in the ninth grade. He will take his exam in December.
— How old were you when you married?
= I was 19. My husband is not a relative of mine. I didn't know him before. It was an arranged marriage, arranged by my parents. Actually, I had seen him but I had not spoken to him. He was a neighbor. The boy's family approached

my parents first and, because he didn't have a very good job, my parents weren't very much for the marriage, but I stepped in and said it was hardly fair for them to reject the boy, and they agreed. I guess I had a soft spot for him after all.

− Can you tell me the differences you see between your mother's life and your own?

= My situation is much worse than my mother's, much worse. Although she is old and sick, she is better because my brothers take good care of her. They are in a position to do so, but in my case, we have to scrimp with the little my husband earns. We are eight in the family, and I have two daughters who should be married too. School fees and examination fees are expensive, and my son has to have shoes and bus fare. It is very difficult. If my first two had been sons, they might be helping now by earning wages, but the eldest are daughters. I can't send them off to do some sort of casual work, and they must be married soon.

− Did you ever go to school?

= I went for four years. If I had gone to school up to the tenth grade, I would have been a sewing instructor. I like embroidery and sewing, or I would like to have been a teacher like my younger sister. Then I would be earning something like my husband. I wouldn't have all these problems.

− What about your daughters?

= The eldest has gone up to the tenth grade but she can't find decent work. The other one is going to school right now. I think she will get through the tenth grade all right. I may be under a lot of difficulties, but I am determined to give my children the best education I can afford so that they won't be in the situation I am in.

− What do you think is the ideal family size given the economic difficulties of today?

= It depends on the income. If a couple gets a fairly big income, they can support a maximum number of children—but definitely not more than four because, even if you earn a thousand rupees a month, you will not be able to support the children or give them benefits. The ideal number is two or three. I would definitely advise my daughters, considering the present situation, to have two or a maximum of three and then stop at that.

– How would you advise your daughters that they limit their families?

= Well, it's not like before. There are ways of controlling pregnancies now. If you go to the district medical officer you can find out, or certainly they can undergo a tubectomy. So there are ways and means now. There are the pills and the IUD, so they could use any of those things. I have an IUD right now.

– Do you have any side effects from the IUD?

= I used to be quite a heavy woman but after I got this IUD I lost a lot of weight. I became frail. When I have my period, I lose too much blood for about three days. My relatives are angry with me because they say I am ruining my health.

– If you had the opportunity, what would you like most to learn to help you in your life?

= If there was an opportunity like that here, I would go to school and learn sewing. If you know how to sew garments, you can sell them to the nearest shop and earn money.

– Would you have preferred to have been born a boy?

= I have thought of it a hundred times. I would have been much better off. You see, a woman here in Sri Lanka has so many responsibilities to shoulder. She really does. She has all the responsibility in maintaining the family. Even if a child falls sick, it is the mother who takes the child to the hospital; it is not the husband. If she were born a man, there would not be all these responsibilities.

If you are a man you can just go from place to place, you get a job, you get paid a monthly salary, and come back and give it to the wife and go off again. But she has to account for the children at home, especially if they are grown daughters. They are under her custody. If a child is going to school, something might happen to him, so until the child returns home, you are on pins and needles. This kind of uneasiness, no peace of mind, all these things would not have happened to me if I had been born a man.

But somehow I have to make us keep going. I keep biting my lips and trying to keep up courage. Somehow, I will see that the children at least come out well in this life.

KURUNEGALA

Under the land reform policy of Sri Lanka, large privately owned estates were nationalized and converted to cooperative management. Some are operated by those who worked them before nationalization; others were turned over to new cooperative groups. Many young people were attracted by the opportunity to live and work on these farms.

A train ride northeast to Kurunegala district enabled me to visit two of these estates. One, the Dambakanda settlement, is managed by young people. They elect their leaders, decide their rules, and operate the plantation. Thirty-nine people tend the coconut palms, banana trees, and sheep, on the farm's 25 acres. They receive five rupees a day and share the annual profits at year's end. Of the people who greeted us, most were in their twenties; some looked even younger.

A young pregnant woman volunteered to talk with us first. She was tall and heavy set. Her pregnancy was just beginning to reshape her body. Confident and smiling, she told us she was a Buddhist, 22 years old, and had been married just eight months before.

— How did you happen to come to this cooperative?
= When I finished school, I trained for two years at a poultry farm. I passed the exam and then joined a rural women's organization. We had had some labor problems on the job, and I knew employment was going to be ended. I heard about this coop and came to be interviewed.
— Did your parents approve of your joining?
= At the start they were reluctant to send me alone. They thought I could find more suitable work than on this farm. Later they found out it is a safe place. They have no objections now.
— How did you meet your husband?
= Here on the farm. After coming here, we got friendly, and the rules say that if you get friendly, it is best to marry. It was a love match.
— Do you think "love matches" are better than marrying the traditional way?
= If my daughter gets proposals from boys, I will ask her

opinion. If she is not agreeable and there is another, she will choose as she wishes.

– Have you and your husband thought about how many children you would like to have?

= I want to have two or three. When the family is small, you can earn what the family requires. There are ways to plan for smaller families. I have read books; I found that in books.

– Did you ever talk with anyone about this or hear about it on the radio?

= No.

– What differences can you see between your mother's time and now?

= The earlier generation, of course, did not have all the opportunities that we have now, mainly education, health, transportation and so on, but economically they were far better off, it seems, because the earlier generation's income was sufficient to meet all their requirements. Now, economically, we earn much more than our parents earned but the cost of living is so high we're not living a happy life. It is difficult. We get more opportunities to show our capabilities in sport activities or in cultural activities and so on. And even without the consent of our parents, we can take an active part in public affairs and political matters.

– Tell me, what do you want for your children, in their lives?

= I want my children to be on a better footing than I am, not this type of life, something better technically. Actually, I want my children to be in a better situation than I am in.

The Serapee Coop Settlement was a larger domain. Its workers were older couples who had worked the estate when it had been privately owned prior to land reform. The coop manager was willing to excuse a dozen women from work, enabling us to meet and talk with them. We sat on the veranda of the old farmhouse, a dozen women dressed in their work saris, a bit ill-at-ease for the first 10 minutes. I talked slowly, once again explaining why I was visiting them. Around us the usual activity of the farm continued; we could see workers coming and going to the day's assigned chores.

When I asked for volunteers to talk further a short wiry woman with a high-pitched voice told me of her life:

= I am 38 years old, I was married at 19, and I have given birth to 11 children. Only 7 still live; the others died at birth. My children are here on the farm. My husband works here also. The oldest son is 21; he, too, is a member of the coop.
– Do you think that your life is much different from your mother's?
= My life is more difficult. The good spices have run out, and the prices paid are not so high. My parents were laborers also but they didn't have such a difficult time. They had only three in their family. I have more children so it is more difficult.
– If you were starting all over again, what do you think is the ideal number of children per family?
= About two or three. It is more difficult when you have many children, so if I were to go back to the marriage age, 18 or 20, I would rather have two or three children. I would take pills or contraceptives.
– How did you first hear about contraceptives?
= Through the village council, about two or three years back.
– Have you ever used contraceptives?
= No.
– Can you describe your work day for me?
= I get up at 4:30 to do the cooking at home. I have to prepare the lunch for the children who go to school and prepare their breakfast. I come here at 6:30. The secretary gives us instructions on what we must do for the day. He decides this according to what the Development Committee decides to do during the season. We have different teams—a team for poultry, a team for dairy, and so on—so we go to our work place. At 11:30 we go for lunch. I go home to do the housework and prepare lunch for the family. I go back to work at 12:30 and continue until 4:00, then I go home, take a bath, rest a bit, and start preparing dinner. I have also to watch the children's homework.
– Do you have any leisure time?
= Sometimes I do mending or sewing. I read the newspa-

per when it comes. I like to listen to our radio. I like agricultural programs.
— Did you ever think it would have been better to have been a man?
= I would have liked to have been a man because of the home problems. My husband ignores so much of the daily problems with home life. And to be born a woman is a sin. This is the religion, you see. Those who are born as a woman are those who have done a thousand sins in a previous life.
— What religion are you?
= Buddhist. To be born a man is a privilege. Whatever a man can do, a woman can do, but it is a privilege to be born a man. According to Buddhist beliefs, I can't say that a woman is better than a man, but a woman can do whatever a man can do.

NEAR KANKESANTURAI, A FISHING VILLAGE

As the train worked its way north past Anuradhapura, the scene was one of desolation. We had traveled out of the lush Colombo region in the early morning. Half way to the northernmost point on the island of Sri Lanka, we were in a different world. The rains hadn't come in nearly four years. Meter-high trunks of dead palm or banana trees stood blackened by the sun. Now and then we could see small huts made of branches and palm leaves, stuck together with a bit of mud. But few people were visible, just the carcasses of trees: mile upon mile of dead nature. When the train stopped at the occasional station, it was boarded by tiny children. Some sold homemade cookies; most were schooled in the art of begging. They wait each day for the trains to pass, stretching out their hands and their hopes. It was late July; the monsoon had again forgotten this vast stretch of earth. Greater misery awaited its people.

The train left me at Kankesanturai station, just a few miles north of Jaffna town. The people there are of Tamil (South Indian) origin. For centuries they have crossed the Palk straits in search of a better life on the coast of Ceylon. White sand beaches stretch for miles on either side of the town. But only an occasional fisherman, alone with his net, adds life to the lonely coastline.

As it happened, I was to have a talk with the wife of one of those fishermen. It was sundown. The local people were spreading their catch to dry on vast canvasses before their homes. We were taken into a family courtyard off the main alley of the village. Inside we found 20 people: six or seven adults, two or three adolescent boys, and children of all ages. This was one family. Conversation was difficult. Everyone wanted to talk to the foreign visitor. The children wanted to sing. When I played their songs back to them from the recorder, everybody else wanted to sing as well. The mother of the family sat close to me so that we could hear each other amid the tumult. She was small, about 40, and incredibly frail looking. Worn and tired, she sighed as she talked. And yet somehow she glowed with a resilience that the interpreter and I both noted.

    — Can you tell me if there is much difference in the way you live and the way your mother lived?
    = Yes, debts, debts. I am suffering much more than my mother. I have lots of debts. I have nine children.
    — At what age did you marry?
    = Sixteen. I don't know when I was born but someone told me I was 16 when I married.
    — What age is your oldest child?
    = Twenty-two years old. The youngest is this one, on my breast.
    — Do you want more children?
    = My horoscope says I will have only nine children. I am satisfied this way. I won't have any more because the horoscope says only nine. I am depending upon fate. I have heard that there are ways to do unnatural things. Some people have done it but they are complaining of ailments.
    — What kinds of ailments?
    = Vaginal discharge, clotting. And some people are afraid—

She shook her head, again and again.

    = You know, there was a case here in my village. A husband had been using this . . . condom . . . whenever he went with his wife. But he was working away from the village. When he came three or four months later, his wife did not have the menses; she was expecting. There was big family trouble. The husband said, "Without me? I was away for four months, so how did you conceive?"

At this point, a young woman pushed her way close to us, disregarding the hubbub and the shoving children. She hesitated, then said:

= Can you tell me about family planning?
– Who are you?
= I am the wife of this woman's son. I am 18. We have been married one year. I had a child but it died. My husband and I want to know about family planning. We don't want to have so many children.

As we left the hut, I thought about meeting these two generations: mother-in-law and young bride, past and present, one depending on her horoscope, the other boldly asking how to find help.

VI TUNISIA

"You find that even today the women who come to family planning services already have 6, 7, or 8 children. They are tired, worn out. They come because they can't cope with more children. But we should have been able to reach them, help them, much earlier."

Fathia M'Zali[1]

It had been 10 years since I last visited this tiny Moslem nation perched on the coast of North Africa at a point where civilizations traveling west from the Middle East have collided with its white beaches for centuries on end. By nature, and by necessity, Tunisians are a hospitable people.

The streets of the capital are far more crowded now than they were before. Gone are the tiny white *voilettes* that once draped the faces of the *tunisoises*. Only a sort of cape—almost a shroud—worn over the heads of the older women remains of the purdah tradition. Young women and teenage girls are seen strolling with young men in the streets, a sight that still can bring protesting comments from the older generation.

In fact, "keeping up with youth" is Tunisia's pressing problem. Of a total population of 5.5 million, 43.2 percent is under the age of 15. One-fifth of the population attends school. As Mme. Fathia M'Zali, president of the National Union of Tunisian Women, points out, "We don't have enough trained adults to guide or teach our youngsters. Education has progressed so

[1]President, National Union of Tunisian Women, interviewed May 11, 1976, Tunis.

that children are better educated than their parents. Yet they need guidance and supervision . . ."

Since its independence in 1956, Tunisia has improved its educational facilities immeasurably and, more importantly, provided a legal base for the advancement of its people. Within five months of Tunisian independence, the National Assembly passed the Personal Status Code, a law that became the foundation for the participation of all citizens in Tunisian society. Polygamy was abolished, repudiation of wives was outlawed, and the marriage age for boys and girls was codified—now 19 and 17 respectively. The personal and active support of President Habib Bourguiba hastened the acceptance of these "modern" ideas. In countless speeches, he spoke out against the veil; he chastised those who impeded the advancement of women.

As a small nation with few natural resources, Tunisia soon took a serious look at the population growth rate and its demands on the developing economy. A national family planning program was launched by the government over ten years ago. In 1973, with the help of the United Nations Fund for Population Activities (UNFPA), an autonomous Office of Family Planning was established under the tutelage of the Ministry of Health. The staff of the Office Nationale du Planning Familial (ONPF) is young, well-trained, and committed to its task. Wherever I traveled throughout the country, local cadres and medical personnel spoke respectfully of the work of the ONPF. It keeps excellent statistical records, produces films, initiates radio programs, and has a dynamic team of field workers.

By joining the efforts to include women in the development of the country to those of the National Family Planning Program, Tunisia seems to have touched a responsive chord in the hearts and minds of its women. Change, here, is positive.

50 KILOMETERS WEST OF SFAX

We had stopped to ask directions several times. It was late in the morning and we were on the way to visit a training center in a village of the Sfax governorate. Centres de la Formation de la Jeune Fille Rurale are found in every region of the country. Their purpose is to train uneducated rural girls in skills that will enable them to earn a living, either within their homes or in village industries. Rug-making, sewing, embroidery, leather work and literacy courses are offered to hundreds of young women each year through a network of training centers. The teachers are barely older than the students and, like them, are from modest rural backgrounds. The local volunteers of the National Union of Tunisian Women provide supervision and administrative support to each center. One such volunteer was with us that morning.

After a few more turns, we arrived at the gate of a huge building, dating back to French colonial times, surrounded by a twelve-foot high wall. It looked too much a fortress to be a center for young women, but inside, within a few moments, girls and women from age 12 to 25 were gathering, with quiet excitement, in a large meeting room. All were dressed in smock-like dresses made by the students of the preceding year. Each class learns to sew, weave, and embroider, and while so doing, makes uniforms for those who will follow.

We talked as a group for half an hour or so until several young women volunteered for personal interviews. In the company of the interpreter, the students talked freely. Flies buzzed. But we forgot insects, the time, our hunger, and those who waited outside, as we listened to the stories of these students' lives.

The first was a heavy-set girl of 19. She sat at my side, facing the interpreter, and smiled hesitantly from time to time. She told us she was from a rural district not far from this village. She had two brothers and two sisters. Neither her mother nor her father had been to school; she had attended classes for two years as a child.

    — Why did you stop?
    = At the time, I chose to stop. Why? Just because I wanted to. Now I regret it. I realize that education is important and has its advantages. But by the time I realized this, I was grown up, and that is why I wanted to come here to this center, to get a bit of education, to help myself.
    — What do you think is the difference between your life and those of your mother or grandmother?
    = Oh, there's a big difference between them. They didn't

have a chance to learn anything. Women were not educated. They were ignorant. They didn't know anything, and
colonialism didn't permit them to go out or about. Today
women are educated. President Bourguiba gave us our
freedom. Today we know our rights. We know our responsibilities.

Before, women didn't have the possibility of choosing
their husband. Husbands were imposed upon them. A
young girl now has the right to choose.

– Can you tell me what qualities you want to find in a
husband?

= I want my husband to be well-mannered and have a good
future. I don't want him to be severe with me. I don't want a
man who closes his wife up in the house. I hope he will let
me work, let me go out. I want to continue to work so that
we can build our happiness together.

– Do you know how many children you would like to have
when you marry?

= Three or four maximum.

– Why not more?

= If there are more it will be difficult to educate them. I
wouldn't be able to take care of them properly. I want them
to be correct, educated, well-mannered. I don't want many.
I will use family planning.

– Did you ever wish you had been born a boy?

= Of course. I would have liked to have been a man. A man
works. He is at ease. He can participate in the defense of his
country. But now it is different even for women. Some are
like men; they are educated. They work in the administration, everywhere. There is no difference anymore.

– If you believe things are so different now, what would
you say is the biggest change in your life?

= I've had the opportunity of coming here to learn. I've
been able to listen to the radio. The radio is a big change. I
like to listen to theatrical programs and plays, or to programs about family planning, marital problems, and forced
marriages. I like the news too. It opens my mind. It gives
me the opportunity to learn what is happening elsewhere.

– Is there a story you could tell us about something you
think has particularly influenced you or made you the person you are today?

= I don't think I should tell about it.

The girl seemed nervous. But after several minutes of patient encouragement, she said:

= Well, there is something which *has* marked my existence. I love a man and my father won't let me marry him. He is not a member of our family, and my parents want me to marry within the family. They say that his work is not a good profession. I have known him since we were children. One day he declared his love for me and said he would go to my parents and ask for my hand. I confided in my mother and she told my father. He absolutely refused to listen. That is really why I came to this center, because I wanted to get away from my family. I was frightened. My father has threatened to disown me if I marry this man. Still now, this fellow hopes we will marry, but my father refuses.
− What will you do if your father continues to refuse?
= Well, if he comes to accept this marriage, all the better. If he continues to refuse, I will be obliged to resign myself and give up hope of marrying him. I am afraid of my father's curse.
− Do you know the man your father has chosen for you?
= Yes, he's a cousin. I don't like him.

By now the young woman was visibly upset. She twisted in her chair. Her eyes reddened. She had told us a secret that she had hidden even from her teachers.

− Let's imagine that one day you are in a position of responsibility like your teachers here. What would you like to do for the women around you?
= First, I would educate them, teach them how to work, teach them sewing, embroidery, handicrafts. I want them to be useful. The Tunisian woman has her problems. She wants to be educated, she wants to have work, wants to be useful. This isn't only Tunisian women. Women in general seek education, openings in their lives. They seek to be useful.

She continued excitedly:

= Women mustn't compare themselves to others, or look back to see how their mothers lived. They must look to the future and seek to improve it.

When the next girl entered, she endeared herself to me immediately. She was plump, almost matronly, and had bright red cheeks. She sat down on the edge of the chair, and throughout our conversation, I noticed, she never sat back but rocked back and forth as we spoke.

— From what region are you?
= My family lives on the outskirts of Sfax but they are country people. We have only been in Sfax a short time. I am 18 years old, and I have four sisters and two brothers.
— Can you tell us about your mother's life and how it differs from yours?
= The difference is that my mother was married off at a very young age. They put her into the hands of her husband and there she was. She had to obey everything. She had nothing. That was in colonial times. Now we are an independent country. We enjoy many freedoms that our mothers knew nothing about. Before, women only went out of the house to gather olives or work in the fields, and they were wrapped up in the traditional costume. Luckily now we have left that behind, and we have abandoned the veil.
— How did you happen to come to this center?
= My sister encouraged me to come here. She even registered me. It was my brother who opposed it. He kept me from coming for a long time because he is very suspicious. He doesn't want his sisters to be emancipated. My mother convinced him by saying this center was very isolated and that I wouldn't risk anything here. I would not be in danger. That was the most important argument. Then my sister and my mother registered me and told my father that it was a very good thing. They convinced him that I would learn a trade. He wanted me to be able to earn a living, and he always kept saying, "What will I do with you if you can't earn anything?"
— Did you ever go to school?
= I went for three years but since I was the eldest daughter of the family they needed me at home. They counted on me

for the housework. Between housework, school work, and the teacher's punishments—she often gave me a hundred lines to copy at night—when I went back home, I lost my head with all the things to do. I fell more and more behind until the day I was so discouraged I didn't return to school.

I am not happy. I have suffered a lot to be in this situation. Since I have no education, I am incapable of doing anything. I am closed within what the others call "ignorance." Since I am the eldest daughter, I prepare the food at home. The others poke fun at my ignorance and tell me I don't even know how to cook. Sometimes I just go away and cry by myself. If I ever meet anyone who treats their daughter like I've been treated by my parents, I will counsel them to give their daughter more freedom, to let her take advantage of her rights. President Bourguiba gave women their rights. They must take advantage of it. I hope my daughter will be well-educated. I will do the impossible to see that she gets a good education. I will even be willing to lie a bit and pretend that I'm educated so that people would listen and accept my daughters in school. I want my daughters to be equal to men. There is no question about it. They will be equal to men. There's no reason why not. I'm sure they will be just as capable as a man.

− If you were in a position to help women, what would you like to do for them?

= I've suffered a lot because I am a girl. I always wanted to be a boy because I was not able to go to school and because my brother mistreated me. He controls everything I do, and he keeps me from going out. Even though I live in Sfax, I never visited the town. I don't know what Sfax looks like. Of course there are women who are aware and educated, and there are others who have no education at all, who are unaware and unawakened. I would push them to develop themselves. I would wake them up and pull them out of their ignorance. I pity them because they are bound to their life of child bearing. They have so many children, so much work and responsibilities.

One of the most important things to teach women is family planning. Teach them to have only two children so that they can educate them, dress them properly, give them everything they need. We must teach women how to help their husbands and help them carry the load of life together.

The young woman hesitated a moment, thought some more, looked up at us and continued:

= One should educate the women who have remained closed up at home without any contacts with the outside. Teach them to educate their children. Teach them to never give a daughter to a man she doesn't know or doesn't love. That is the way to assure a good life, a better life, a better future for them.
　　Look at my closed life. Although I live in a big city like Sfax, I came here from one prison (the home) to another prison, here in this remote village (the center). When I return to Sfax, I will go back to the first prison. If ever I marry, I will go into a third prison (the husband's home). I will never be able to enjoy life like most girls, dressing up, going out walking, or just having fun.

I took the girl's hand in mine. It was cold and calloused by work. She was not crying. On the contrary, she was quite in possession of herself. It was the two visitors who were made uncomfortable by her words. We talked for a time about the possibilities of her future, that she should not think that her life was without hope. She might be able to find work in her home first, then convince her father and brother that she was capable of having employment outside the home. Finally I said:

– We will all be old one day. What is it you would like people to say about you when you are an old woman?
= I try to be as nice as possible in my life, as helpful as possible. I mustn't humiliate anyone. I must be hospitable to all people whether they are superior to me or inferior to me. I try to do everything which will make people like me.

LA HENCHA

In the distance we could see a large group of women waiting near a small building. We stopped the car and learned the building housed a weekly health clinic. As we entered, we were jostled by the Bedouin women who were anxious to get medicine or advice, and then return to their work in the fields. Originally a nomadic people, some have been given land by the Tunisian government and have chosen to settle in this area. Others are still nomads and migrant laborers. The men are shepherds; the women work for day wages in the fields. That morning, the women were a colorful group; they had obviously decorated themselves for the visit to the clinic. Their dark eyes were circled with *Khol*, their cheeks reddened, and most wore what appeared to be a recently acquired *meliah*, a dress held together by the traditional silver brooches of the Bedouins. They wore bright turbans and most were tattooed—tiny spots between the eyebrows or a series of lines upon the cheeks.

When a young male nurse came to greet us, we asked if it would be appropriate to meet with some of the women. The nurse smiled and granted permission, shouting to all that they should gather around for an explanation of our visit.

We crowded into a room of women and infants, explained the object of our visit, and suggested that anyone who wished to talk with us should follow us out of the building.

Out we went, amid giggles, pats, shouts, and shoving. A dozen women followed us to the steps of the clinic. Real difficulty lay in selecting a few among them, disappointing the others. Once the choice was made, we took our first "volunteer" across the road to the center of a large field. There we sat in the shade of a single olive tree. We could view the empty fields for yards around us; certainly, privacy was assured.

The morning was hot and the earth had turned to near-cement from lack of rain. We sat cross-legged, myself, the interpreter, and a strong, almost husky, 40-year old woman. Like the others, she had tattooed arms and face. Her smile was warm and gay.

— How many children do you have?
= Ten, seven boys and three girls. I was married when I was 15. I had a baby every year. My oldest is now 22, the youngest 12 and 5 months. I have been wearing an IUD for the past seven months.
— Does it bother you at all?
= No, I am happy to wear it.
— How did you first hear about family planning?
= I'm from another region and heard that there were things

you could put inside the uterus. When I came here, I took my sick child to the clinic one day and the nurse there offered to place an IUD. I said to myself, "Why not, instead of having a child every year." It will help us get out of our humiliating existence. It helps us get out of our misery, to get out of having a child every year.

I would have preferred to have less children, anyway. When I think of all the things that I ate, or swallowed, hoping they would prevent me from having another child! But they didn't work, and now it is better. All the women are happy that there are these methods to help them find better health and even help them nurse their babies.

– What were these traditional methods you mentioned, these methods of birth control?

= Castor oil leaves and other plants. Many women use magic, like the baby's dried umbilical cord. When it has fallen from the child, you soak it in water, and then stuff it with a very bitter powder. I don't know the name but it is very bitter to taste, and then you hang the cord either on the mother's ear or around her neck. That way they think they will not get pregnant again. It is a custom; it's magic.

– All right, tell me how many children would you like to have had?

= Oh, I wanted six children but I have ten. I would have liked three boys and three girls.

– Do you talk about family planning with your friends and your husband or your daughters?

= I never talk with men about it. No one ever talks about it with men but with other women, yes. We educate each other. We help each other mutually.

– But if women don't have a child every year, don't the men begin to ask some questions?

= Yes, there are some husbands who are not aware that their wives practice family planning. The women do it in secret. In the beginning I didn't tell my husband.

Can you imagine, if you take one hundred men you could probably only find one who would not agree that his wife stop having children, right? Well, I had to get that one man in a hundred. He did not want me to use a contraceptive method. He said, "It isn't normal for you to stop what is destined to exist. Given the fact that you have a potential existing in you for a certain number of children, you must have them. You must let them come into the world. You don't have the right to prevent this potential from existing. You are like a chicken with a certain number of eggs to lay. You must have them. It would be a sin to stop nature's phenomenon."

I just told him I couldn't take it anymore because my health was not good enough to go on having children year after year.

– Do you think your husband's attitude has its origin in his religious beliefs?

= Yes. He is a very religious man. He thinks it is a sin to stop having children.

– But do you think it's a sin?

= Absolutely not. What is important for me is my health. It is important that I be light and free, that I be able to go where I please, that I be strong enough to work and care for the family.

– Do you associate family planning with the general health care of women?

= Family planning is a very good thing because when the woman is pregnant or when she nurses she's always tired, very tired. She's not in good health. Having children keeps her from going to ceremonies, to marriages. When she doesn't have any children she is much lighter. She can go anywhere. A large number of children prevent her from doing her work. She is obliged to help with the harvest and work in the field, and when she has a child, she has to take care of the child's needs, clean it, feed it, and consequently the mother is always handicapped.

– You said you had a daughter of 22. Have you discussed family planning with her? Does she know how many children she would like to have?

= My daughter was married four years ago and she already has a little boy, but I certainly wouldn't talk about family planning with her or with any of my daughters. Never. We never discuss things like that with our daughters. It is a question of modesty.

– But if one day your daughter had six or seven children wouldn't you counsel her to use a contraceptive?

= No, she can just go and ask the people of her own age.

We talk with those of the same age but not with our daughters.

Conversations with several women followed, there, under the olive tree. During the morning, I observed a woman working in the field a few hundred feet away. As the day wore on, I noticed her work brought her closer and closer to us. When the last woman had left, she strutted over to the interpreter and me. "You certainly are the lucky ones," she said, "to be educated, to be there just talking with people, while I am here gathering straw in the field."

These words were not spoken aggressively but with a tinge of bitterness. I asked if she had time to sit with us for a moment; she smiled at the invitation and joined us.

She was 36 years old but looked much older and frail in comparison to the other women we had seen. Her arms were too slender, too delicate. The *meliah* she wore was worn and dirty; it was held together with safety pins. Such pins are a sign of poverty in the Sahel, where the Bedouin women wear their silver jewelry at all times, for safekeeping and as a display of relative wealth. Since this woman was wearing none, she no doubt possessed none.

Amid the sound of bleating sheep that had followed her to our tree, we learned that she had been married to a cousin at age 13, that she had three sons and three daughters, and that two other children had died. One was stillborn; the other died shortly after birth. She told us that she had an IUD placed following the birth of her last child eleven years before; and later she'd had a tubectomy. She smiled incessantly. Pride in her audacity to thrust herself upon us pleased her more, I suspect, than the conversation we shared.

    — How did you first hear about family planning?

    = I was waiting for some medicine in the dispensary one day when a nurse came and talked with us. He told us about contraceptive methods. For some time I had wanted to use a contraceptive method so I took the opportunity to have an IUD placed. The rest of the women fled but I spoke up and said I would have one.

    — What did your husband say about the tubectomy operation?

    = My husband even went with me when I had it done. He encouraged me. All the other women were making fun of me. They even scolded me for doing it but I really didn't care. I just decided to have it done and I did. What good is it to have so many children? We have such small financial means, besides if the sterilization operation had existed a long time ago I would have had my tubes tied after just two children.

− But why did the other women make fun of you, or make a mockery of your situation?

= Well, in those days it was a rare thing, but you know by the time I went to the hospital everyone wanted to come and see me. They came to visit and see this extraordinary thing.

− And what about those women now? Have they changed? Do they plan their families?

= Yes, there are women around who plan their families, who go the good route, but there are others who haven't understood, unfortunately for them. You see, before we lived the life of beasts. Today we thank God that all women are freed; whoever needs to go somewhere can just go. No one bothers them anymore. Nothing is exceptional in these times.

− You said earlier that we were fortunate to be educated. If you had been able to go to school, what would you have wanted to do?

= If I had gone to school, I would have wanted to open my mind above all, to open my mind, educate others, help others, and learn everything. I want to learn about everything.

− Do your daughters go to school?

= Yes, they go to school and I want them to go just as far as they can, to the limit of their talents.

− Do you want your daughters to get married at age 13?

= Certainly not. Anyway, that happened in other times. Now it no longer exists. Seventeen is a good age or even older. You know, I didn't even have my menstruation when I was married. I got it a month after my marriage and right then I became pregnant. I want my daughters to have time to finish school, to prepare their trousseau, to prepare their wedding.

− Tell me the difference between the lives of women before and your life now.

= Oh, it is better now. Today, the men are better than

before because they are educated, they are understanding, they are kind, and they understand the rights of men and the rights of women. We have mutual respect between the husband and the wife. The husband wants his wife to look well. Before, a man could divorce his wife but now he can't. She could be beaten, but today that is no longer true. The woman of today is much better and that is because of Bourguiba.

A SHEIK'S HOME

As we drove north toward Tunis, mile upon mile of olive trees lined either side of the road. Towns and plantations compete for land in this densely populated Sahel region.

The interpreter with me that morning was a social worker from the area. When we came to one of the numerous roadside markets, she stopped the car, got out, and started toward a run-down store, something between a barber shop and a grocery store. A tall elderly man came out to greet her. He wore the woolen *cashabia* of the region. He was introduced as the village sheik or chief, a highly respected man in this area. He is illiterate but his sons are university graduates. One is a lawyer, the other an engineer. When he was told of our mission, he invited us to his home for "a talk with my women. There are three, my wife, my daughter-in-law, and a daughter. They will talk with you."

Guided by the sheik, who joined us in the car, we drove off the main road, around a few buildings, to find a large house which appeared to be 10-15 years old. A wrecked automobile, carts, and old tires littered the front yard. Inside we sat in a neat and cheerful sitting room furnished with a couch, armchairs, a coffee table with a vase of plastic flowers. Pictures decorated the walls of the cool room. Once the sheik had introduced us and departed, the women served lemonade. Then, one by one, they sat with us to be questioned and to question in return.

The eldest, the sheik's wife, wanted to be the first to talk. She was wearing the traditional country *meliah*, a turban, and silver bracelets. She was tattooed on forehead, hands, and arms like most women her age. The tattoos simulate jewelry and are considered part of one's attire, just as makeup is in some Western countries.

It was barely necessary to ask her questions. Once she

understood the object of our visit, she was eager to tell her story. She told us she had no idea of her age. "Someone figured it out once to be roughly about 67," but she was not sure. She didn't know her eldest son's age either, replying, "You'll have to ask his father. He has all the certificates."

= You see, I don't read. I'm not educated. I don't know how to read or write so how would you expect me to know such things? I have five sons and three daughters. The last daughter is 22 or 23, I think. She had to get a birth certificate to work, and I remember her telling me she was about that age.
− Tell me what differences you see between your life and those of your daughters.
= My daughters are all fine. They know so much more than I do. There's a big difference between my life and theirs. I couldn't even go to town in my day. Now my daughters go about here and there. We didn't get to meet our husbands until we were married. They just gave us a husband we didn't know. Of course I have learned things also during these new times. I kept hearing things around me so I began to learn hygiene, how to better care for my children, how to give them an education different from my own. We all began to imitate each other, and that is how we changed our old habits. Nowadays it is much better, better at all levels.
− What brought about these changes?
= It was Bourguiba. Where else do you think it comes from? Now women are free. They can go where they want. Men can't say anything. They can't keep women from doing what they want. Women are free, and women are just as capable as men. They are equal.

Not the likes of me. I live like a beast. I'm not educated. Since I don't know anything, it is obvious that I'm always left behind, overtaken by the menfolk. But I'm happy to see other women are not like me. Before, women were always in a weak state. They weren't healthy. They gave births at home, and now they can go to a hospital. They come and take her and she's in a clean place. She enjoys it all. Now she can enjoy everything—freedom, cleanliness, good health.

— What do you think of family planning? Do you think it's a good idea? Does it aid the health of women?

= Yes, of course. I've heard all about it and all the young people do it, this family planning. One has an IUD, another takes the pill, another has a tubal ligation. We didn't know anything like that before. I would have done it if it had been available. It's much better to live that way than the way we did.

— How many children do you think is good for a family in these times?

= A small number is much better because you can feed them better, nurse them better, clothe them well and see that they are clean.

— Do you talk with other women about family planning?

= Of course. That's all we talk about.

— And what do you think men think about all this? Do they perceive much change. Do they like it?

= If they don't like the change, it's just too bad. We are equal now. If they aren't happy about it, there's nothing they can do against change. It is the same for all the women in the world, not just the women here in Tunisia. All women are seeking to learn, to go out, to dress properly. All women want to listen and to become better people.

When we had finished philosophizing about the general state of the world and the women therein, I asked if she would permit us to talk with her daughter-in-law. She seemed flattered by our interest in her family, and called her daughter-in-law into the room to take her place.

The daughter-in-law was 40 years old. She wore a Tunisian style dress but it showed the influence of European tailoring. Her hair was tied back with a ribbon; she wore no jewelry. She had been married at the age of 14 and had not known her husband before the wedding. Her first menstrual cycle came a month after her wedding. She gave birth a year later. She has seven children.

— Do you want more children?

= No, I'm planning my family. I started after the birth of my last daughter nine years ago. For five years I had an IUD but it didn't work well. I stopped. Now I use the calendar method.

– Would you have wanted to "plan" earlier had you known about it?

= Yes, of course. I would have spaced my children four years apart, but family planning didn't exist in those days. Even my children complain about me having so many of them. My eldest son kept saying, "These last children are too many. You should have stopped at four." I would have liked to use a method since about the fourth child. That is why I began telling other women about family planning when I learned about it. I am active in the Women's Union, and I give lectures about family planning. I say, "I couldn't help having seven children but now you can choose." Now that my children are grown, that is what I do. I teach women hygiene and health. I tell them about family planning and how useful it is not to have so many children.

– And what does your husband think about this?

= He agrees. My husband always wished we could stop having so many children. We are definitely of the same opinion, and my children too. I talk about this with my daughters. Once, one of the younger children said, "Why don't you have another baby, Mother?" The older one shouted back, "That is enough! We have too many already. Enough!"

I have a sister who is married and has four children. She gets along well with her husband, and she has stopped having children completely. She had herself sterilized. She is very happy about it. She takes care of her four children, dresses them properly, educates them, raises them with good manners. Everyone has heard these things on the radio and on television. They know better these days than to have so many children.

– You agree with family planning but I want to know what you think about abortion.

= I don't think it's bad. In fact, once I was terribly tired and I was pregnant. I just couldn't continue. I just couldn't have another child so at that time I had a curettage. I think it is good when necessary.

– Did you ever go to school?

= No, I only have the knowledge of the Koran, but if I had been able to be like the girls of today, I would have liked to help other people, to help educate them, orient them, show them the best way. As it is now, I have to ask my children to explain things to me, things I don't understand on the radio, for example. When they explain, I can understand, but I would like to be like men, go to meetings and do serious work, do what I am capable of doing. That's what we women would like to do, serious work like the men.

– Was there ever any time in your life when you wished you had been born a boy?

= I always wished it. Every time I was in conflict with my husband, I wanted to be a man so I could do as he does, be able to do that which, theoretically, I was unable to do. I wanted to go beyond men.

It is the lack of education which left me in this situation. There is such a difference between those who are educated and those who are not. I try very hard to understand everything even though I am not educated at all.

Once I went to France for medical treatment, and I saw women marching in the streets all together. I don't understand French so I don't know what it was all about, but I wanted to go with them. I wanted to be like them. I wanted to participate in what they were doing. I want to go to conferences, lectures, anything where I can learn and bring back the experience to women here. I would like to meet other women to exchange ideas. I want to learn from them, so we can progress here.

More lemonade and home-made cookies were served, and then we talked with the third woman of the family. She is the sheik's first daughter. Only 28 years old, she appears much older, much less energetic, than her 40-year old sister-in-law.

= I have seven children, four boys and three girls. I was married very, very young, at 13. I had my first child at 14, but now I have had a tubectomy because that's enough.

– How did you first hear about family planning?

= I heard it on the radio and from other people, then some social workers came to inform us about family planning. I used two different methods. I had an IUD for a year but it didn't work well; I was sick. Then they prescribed the pills. I swallowed them for about a year but they, too, made me sick. So I put the IUD back. All of a sudden, there I was, pregnant again. I had expelled the IUD from my body, so when the last child was born, they asked me if I wanted to have a tubal ligation. I said, "Yes, it is useless to go any further. I must stop having children."

It is better to have less children. You can dress them better, feed them better, educate them. Family planning is a good thing, especially from the health and rest point of view. Pregnancies are tiring. I would have used the methods long before if I had known about them. In fact, I would have had the sterilization done long before the seven children came. I hope my daughters don't have more than two children. If they do, I will try to stop them.

– What would you say are the major changes you have observed in the last few years?

= Women are not like they were before. We are in a new era. Look at me, I have a brother who is a lawyer, another who is an engineer, and I never went to school. I can do nothing.

Today it is different. Women are educated. They, too, can go out. Now everyone is trying to get ahead, to listen, to learn, and all women want to go forward. They are trying to improve themselves. We are always striving to be better.

LE KEF REGION

It had been raining since we left Tunis. Everything along the road was soggy: people, animals and fields. We passed Roman ruins, rich wheat lands, and hundreds of sheep and cattle tended by raggedly dressed men and boys.

As we drove westward into the mountains near the Algerian border, we could see the tents of the nomads who migrate to Northern Tunisia during the summer months. Here summer days are hot but the nights are cool. Winters are cold and damp and bring snow. The first day in Le Kef began with a visit to a newly-opened clinic. The government had bought a former commercial building and was remodeling it to create a multi-service maternal and child health clinic. The first ward to be completed specializes in tubal ligation. The sparsely furnished rooms were a model of cleanliness and gaiety; the walls were painted white and the windows were outlined by light blue curtains. Each patient wore a similar night dress, bathrobe, and slippers. The administrator had requested additional funds enabling him to make gifts of the "uniforms" when the patients leave the clinic. He believes the outfits would serve as family planning advertisements in villages where bathrobes, slippers, and nightdresses are nonexistent.

Our conversation was with a patient we found propped up in her bed talking with a nurse. She had undergone tubal ligation the day before. She told us her husband is a shepherd, that they are nomads. They take the herd wherever there is grass or, more important, water. She had never been to a hospital before. This was the first time she had slept in a bed. When asked if she would like to talk with us, she replied, "Of course." But her attitude remained one of resignation. As we talked more, I realized the resignation had nothing to do with the subject of our conversation. It was a part of her entire life. Her existence she said, "has no object." She is 35 years old.

— How many children do you have?
= Five living children, six who died. Usually they died before the end of the first year. One would have been nearly 20 if he had lived; the youngest is three. Last year I had a stillborn child, a little girl.
— Did you have any help in delivering those children?
= Sometimes I had a matron help me but other times I delivered alone. During the last birth I had complications and I couldn't deliver the baby. The head kept coming out and, then going back in, so finally they decided to take me to the hospital. I had the baby on the way. I didn't continue on to the hospital. I turned around and went home because the baby was already dead.
— At what age did you marry?
= I was in puberty the year I married. I must have been about 13.
— How did you hear about family planning the first time?
= I don't know what you mean by family planning.

At this point the interpreter broke in and said, "She only knows that women come here to have an operation so that they do not have more children. She doesn't know about contraceptive methods at all. Her sisters told her about this place."

— Did your husband want you to have this operation?

= He agreed but he didn't want me to have it done now. He wanted me to wait until the summer was over because this is the work season. We have to keep moving constantly, but I preferred to come now.

— If you had known about this operation before, would you have wanted to come here earlier?

= I was afraid of God before.

She turned to the interpreter; they talked for some time together. The interpreter explained, "She asked me, 'Would you be able to kill someone?' I answered that it isn't a question of killing anyone but avoiding that someone be unhappy and live a life of misery."

= I don't fear God anymore because now I must stop having children. I just can't have any more and live this way. Another thing is, before, all my children died. So I continued to have children for fear that they would all die.

Again the interpreter and she talked together. The interpreter explained, "I asked her if she knows that the religious leaders here have said that the Koran does not forbid planning one's family, that it is better to have a few children and give them a proper life. The woman replied, 'If I had known that, I would have come here a long time ago.' "

— Do you see any difference in the way you live and the way your mother lived years ago?

= I don't understand my life. I don't gain anything from it. I am always moving about with the herds. Perhaps my mother lived better because she had a place to stay, a home, but it is different for me. I work in the fields and spin wool.

— Do your daughters go to school? What do you want most for them?

= My daughters have never been to school. Only one son has gone but he has to change schools each time we move. I want my children and my daughters to be happy but I haven't been able to send them to school.

— At what age do you want your daughters to marry?

= Well, they won't marry as early as I did. At least they will wait until they are 17 years old as the law says, and they

will choose their husbands even if I don't think the man is good for them.
- Does your husband think the same way?
= My daughters are still young. I haven't discussed it with him. I haven't seen the need to discuss it with him.
- Do you ever have an opportunity to hear radio programs?
= No, we have no radio. Even if I hear a radio, I don't pay any attention. I'm not accustomed to it. There is no need for such things for me.
- Are you glad to have been born a woman or would you have preferred to be a man?

Both the interpreter and the bedridden woman were amused by my question, giggling and commenting in Arabic. Yet a few seconds later the woman became serious once again, speaking excitedly:

= Yes, sometimes when I want my children to go to school, I wish I were a man. I want them to have a good life but my husband is against that kind of project. In moments like this, I think it would have been better to have been a man, to have the possibility, or the means, to help my children get ahead in life.
- Why does he oppose this?
= Because we are poor. We have no financial means because we are constantly moving.
- Do you think women, wherever they may be, have problems in common with each other?
= I feel close to all women. Nearly all women have the same problems.
- If you had been to school as a child, what would you have liked to learn?
= I don't know. Your question is too difficult. I don't want anything. I have nothing to wish for. I am here but this life serves no purpose.

NABEUR

Nabeur is another of the hillside villages that dot the landscape of northwestern Tunisia. We had traveled about 30 kilometers from Le Kef, turning, winding and eventually, bumping along roads of various widths and conditions. We learned there were no "women meetings" scheduled that day. Hence, for interview purposes, the social worker suggested asking village women she knew well if they would like to talk with me. We climbed up the steep hill of the town among chickens, roosters, and barefooted children to knock on the gates of the homemade stone walls that surround each house. The door would open a crack; the social worker would disappear inside for a time, to return with a negative reply. Each woman said that if she had known we were coming she would have asked her husband if it was all right but, "since he isn't here, I can't talk with you without asking him first."

We decided instead to talk with a group of young girls at the local training center. The old, damp rectangle building had just two large rooms on either side of a narrow courtyard. Thirty-five young girls from the surrounding hills were crowded into the dark rooms, learning rug weaving, embroidery, and sewing. They did not board here; they return each afternoon to their homes.

The 19-year old girl recorded here lives in the village. She has never traveled more than a kilometer or two from it. She is considered privileged in comparison with the majority of the students here. They have never been able to attend school as she has.

— How many children in your family?
= Seven, three boys and four girls. I am the third born.
— How did you happen to come here to this center?
= To learn how to work. My parents want me to learn a skill so I can earn money. At first, my father didn't want me to come. He is old-fashioned. Once a girl becomes of age, she must stay at home. He is from a very strict family, and young girls never used to go out of the house before, but I kept asking him. He finally agreed when I told him that when I finish school I must learn a profession. In these times everyone learns how to work, and young girls no longer stay in the house waiting for marriage. This is how he accepted and gave his permission.
— How many years did you go to school?
= Twelve years, and then I had to stop because the higher

level classes were in Le Kef. I would have had to board there because it is too far; that was not possible. I was obliged to just stay at home.

— Can you tell us how your life differs from that of your mother?

= My mother never went to school and she never worked. She married at 16. The life of girls in those days was just to stay in the house and prepare for marriage. That was the goal of all girls, just to get married. But now the goals have changed. You go to school and learn a trade so that you can support yourself. My mother is happy about my life because it is so different from her own. My mother was married to a man she didn't know and was obliged to accept it because her parents wanted it that way. Now it is completely different.

— Did your mother ever see her husband before the wedding?

= No.

— Do you think that your parents are going to let you choose your husband?

= Well, that question has already come up. Someone asked my parents for me. I didn't want him so my parents refused also. I think it is up to me to choose my husband.

— And the day you marry and have children, what would you like for your daughters?

= The first thing is to push them in their studies to the limit of their capabilities. If by chance they can't go far enough to obtain a position in the administration or something similar, then I want them to learn a trade that will permit them to earn a living.

— How many children would you like to have?

= Three.

— Why only three? And how will you possibly be able to limit the number to three?

= I want three children and I will use family planning. I heard about it at the health center. When women go to the dispensary, there are motivators who tell them about it. And there are teams who go from door to door in the village. My mother has used a traditional family planning method. I don't know which one. I think it is something that my mother made herself, but I am pretty sure that my mother doesn't use modern methods.

– At what age do you think you would like to marry?
= I want to get married at 23 or 24.
– What sex do you want your three children to be?
= Two girls and a boy.
– Do you think every child should have the same educa-
tion?
= Yes, it is the same for boys and girls. If they have the
same advantages in education, they are equally capable.
They can do the same work, and they can do it equally well.
– If you had been able to go to school longer, what would
you have liked to be?
= A teacher. If I had been a boy like my brother, I would
have been able to go away to school. My father put my
brother in a boarding school when he finished school in the
village, but that couldn't happen to me.
– And what would you have done if you were a teacher?
= I would try to convince rural women, by my example, of
the importance of study and of the education of their
daughters, also of the importance of family planning because there are still women who don't pay any attention to
it. I would help them learn to organize their homes. I would
try to tell them that even though they "missed the boat" in
their lives because they couldn't go to school, or go out, or
travel, that they must want all that for their daughters. They
must be convinced of it. I want to make myself useful in life
so that when I am gone people will say that I rendered
service, that I did things for them.
– What are the qualities that you want in a husband?
= That he be a good worker. I would like him to be educated. I want him to be an industrious worker, and I want to
work to help him also. I want to have a good understanding
between us. If we do something, we will do it together. We
will ask each other's opinion.
– What would happen if you did not agree one day and he
beat you?
= I would accept it. If we agree on most things, if we are
well together, I would accept it. If a man beats his wife, it is
probably because he asked her to do something and she
didn't do it.
– What if it wasn't her fault? What if the husband is cruel
and egotistical?
= Under those conditions I would leave the house for

awhile. I would stay two or three days with my parents and
then I would forget and go back to him. I would be obliged
to return.

VII MEXICO

"A woman is supposed to be the property of one man: her husband. If she goes to a clinic, another man, the doctor, is going to see and touch her. The husband won't let her go . . . and she, too, is reluctant. This is a great barrier to the acceptance of family planning in Mexico . . ."
Lucia Mier Y Teran de Munoz[1]

A Sunday afternoon visit to Mexico City's Chapultepec Park offers the visitor a visual statement on Mexico's population dilemma. Children, hundreds of children, mostly infants, are paraded in the noonday sun by proud parents. Families of five, six or more children play ball, roll on the grass, or picnic with elder members of the family. But repeatedly, this gay bucolic scene is disturbed by the appearance of ragged peasant women. One has an infant strapped to her back. A 4-year-old clasps her skirt, while a 2-year-old prances along behind, holding the hand of an older sister. They are beggars. They go from one family to another, in hopes of receiving leftovers of the picnic lunches. I saw one tiny child actually dance with joy when the mother of a well-fed family gave her a small loaf of bread.

Modern Mexico is a vast series of contradictions, contradictions that originate, for the most part, in the complex stratification of its social classes. A small upper class enjoys the goods and services provided by a modern international economy while the great majority of Mexicans are excluded from the benefits of economic and social progress. Even the medical services of Mexico are class-oriented. There are hospitals for

[1]Social anthropologist, interviewed February 15, 1977, Mexico City.

government workers, others for the poor and the peasantry, and still others for the wealthy.

Mexico's population has passed the 60 million mark; its growth rate is 3.5 percent, one of the highest in the world. Anthropologists at the National Population Council told me they estimate that 1 million illegal abortions are performed each year in Mexico.

The National Population Council was established by law in 1973; its role, under the Ministry of Interior, is to coordinate population policy among all government agencies. Working with a host of international and bilateral agencies, Mexico has benefited from the counsel and experience of a variety of sources. Yet the central arguments in the population "debate" in Mexico remain very much the same as in 1973: 1) Mexico is a large country and can support a much larger population; 2) population policy is nothing but a North American imperialist plot; and 3) the problem will take care of itself if "we just progress and prosper."

These arguments were mentioned to me by several official sources as bothersome barriers in the way of an effective population policy. One man added, "And the debate is not over yet."

I was also told that the cultural problems are equally complex: 1) women are not accustomed to consulting a (male) doctor; 2) the church has a variety of positions on the population question, some liberal, others opposed to any form of family planning; and 3) *machismo*—the belief in total male dominance—is ever present.

During conversations with rural women, many of these latter factors were mentioned. For this reason, the recent communication campaign of the National Population Council appears strange to some. Its slogan is *"Señora, ud decide si se embaraza."* ("Women, pregnancy is your responsibility.")

SAN SEBASTIAN

Far from the main road in the foothills thirty miles south of Oaxaca, we were welcomed to a Zapotec Indian village. The Land-Rover bumped and strained through a dried riverbed, the only way of reaching San Sebastian.

We spent the morning at the mud-brick home of Maria-Louisa, a woman of 42. Her sister, Sophia, age 40, was visiting her. Both women are short, as are almost all of the Zapotec tribe. Their bodies are solidly built; they work constantly at the hard tasks of the fields and the grueling duties of the home.

The sisters were amused by our visit; they joked and laughed throughout the conversation, making fun of their lives, their menfolk, and of the chores they continued to perform as we spoke together.

The kitchen was a lean-to on the outside wall of the small house. Maria-Louisa cooked tortillas on a large earthen plate, set upon rocks. She constantly fed the fire beneath the plate with corn husks and stalks. There was no chimney, and I mused at how she managed to breathe smoke all morning long without seeming to notice. Throughout our talk, a spindly-legged 2-year old kept returning to her, to pull on her dress or finger the long braids wrapped around her head, demanding yet another brittle, reheated tortilla. I watched the pot she had put on the fire; it took exactly 35 minutes for the water to come to a boil on the homemade stove. Sophia had come to help her sister grind corn meal for the tortilla dough. She remained on her knees for two hours, grinding the small kernels with a rolling pin-like stone placed on a low stone table.

The sisters first wanted to tell about a third sister, Anna, whose situation was the concern of the day. Anna lives next door but was not allowed to join us. Her husband does not let her leave her house. Sophia began telling Anna's story:

= Anna is going to leave her husband because the mother-in-law has been making too much trouble. That mother-in-law has always been against their marriage and she has finally succeeded in splitting them up. They have four children but they didn't even get married until the third child was born. The priest finally said, "If you don't get married, I'm not going to baptize this child." If it wasn't for the words of the priest I think the mother-in-law would have never permitted they marry. I don't know what is wrong with Anna. She wants to go to Mexico City. She is going to leave the children and take only the baby with her. How can she possibly do something like that, go off alone?

Maria-Louisa joined in, saying:

= She can't even come here with us because if her husband comes home and doesn't find her in the house, he says,

"Who do you think gives orders around here, anyway?
Why do you leave to go to your sister's house?" He thinks
that when she goes out men will pass by and look at her. He
beats her and she's often black and blue on the thighs or on
the back. He beats her because his mother is constantly
filling his head with rumors. She is going to leave him and
leave the children with him as well. She wants to go to some
other place, escape. She keeps saying, "I can't live with
him anymore. I can't take all this. Who else would take this
as long as I have?"
— How long have they been together?
= Ten years, a long time. But he has such old-fashioned
ideas, you know. The woman has to be in the house all the
time. She has to confess everything to him. She can't have a
thought of her own. That's all right. You can be jealous, or a
tyrant like that, but at least you have to do your share . . .
You have to bring money and care for your family. The
reason we are against him is because he doesn't fulfill his
part, he doesn't care for the family properly. Anna has to
look for food while he is gallivanting around. That doesn't
make any sense. You know, here, rules are rules!
= Once Anna leaves here she will never come back. That
is what always happens. She will try to find work and if she
finds it, she will never want to come back here to work as
we do, without money, without being able to buy things.

I interrupted the two sisters to ask:

— Do you think life is much different now than in your
grandmother's or mother's time?

Sophia spoke first, saying,

= Our grandmother's life was very difficult. She was left a
widow quite young and had to do all the things that men do.
She had to go to the hills with a machete and cut wood,
loads of it, and she would carry it back to the house herself.
But our lives are pretty much the same as hers. Before,
things were very difficult as far as the work went but
centavos went a long, long way. Money bought much more
then. My grandmother would sell a big squash from the

field and get enough *centavos* to buy all the food she needed to feed her children.

For one *centavo*, one cent, she would get a handful of soap. But we can't buy it because it costs much more now. And before, it would take all day to make the tortillas a household needed. The women's hands were always in the water (used to soak the corn kernels). Their hands would start wearing away. The skin would just peel off.

Maria-Louisa added:

= When our mother was a girl there was a school but she didn't go because they didn't have the money to buy pencils and a notebook. I went to school at eight and stayed for only three years. I didn't learn anything so I stopped. I can write my name and read a little, that's all. Even now, it is the same. The teachers don't live in the villages. You never know when the teacher will come to teach the class. Some days he comes, some days he doesn't, so the children never know what to do and they get disgusted.

If I had been able to go to a good school, I would have liked to learn how to sew clothes so I could earn a bit of money. As it is we are very backward; we don't know anything. I want my daughters to be different from me, have a different life for themselves. I don't want them to be here, on their knees making tortillas, like me. I hope they can study and get the career they want.

− What about you, Sophia? What would you have liked to learn in school?

= I wanted to be a secretary—a bi-lingual secretary. That would permit me to earn money. As it is we women are not worth anything. All the time we are beneath a man, below him, no? You know how men are, they want to order us around all the time.

Even though we work all the time with them, men get the inheritance rights to everything. They get the land, the house, all the animals. Our mother just died but we didn't get a thing. Everything belongs to her husband now . . . and then it will go to our brothers. Women are not equal to men. When you get married, the man says, "I rule, you don't. You can just work and go and get things. I don't want other

people saying you live off me . . . I'm going to live off you."
We can do nothing about it.
– Tell me, at what age did you marry?
= Nineteen.
= Seventeen.
– And how did you meet your husbands?
= We knew each other in school. Then afterwards, when
we left school we would see them when we went out to do
errands. At the river, when we did the washing, we would
see them. The boys would happen to be there and we would
talk with them . . .

Maria-Louisa explained:

= One day my husband just asked me to come and live with
him so I packed my things and went to his house, with his
parents. I was lucky because I married soon; my mother-
in-law liked me very much. She told my husband, "You
should marry this girl." Within a year we were married.

Her situation was different, Sophia said:

= My mother-in-law didn't like me. She didn't want us to
get together so she made a lot of trouble. She wouldn't give
me anything to eat; she wanted to starve me out of the
house. After the first child was born I left and came back to
my mother's house. My husband waited for five years to
come and get me. After another year we got married.

– How many children do you have now?
= Seven.
– And you, Maria-Louisa?
= Ten in all. Six are still in the house; three have married;
another died of measles.
– Do you want to have more children?
= No, life is too difficult now.
– But don't you need children to help you with the field
work, or even in the house?
= No, that is not important anymore. The more children
you have, the more work you have. And we need more land
if we are to have more children. We wouldn't have to work

so much land if we didn't have as many children.

– Then what do you think is a good number of children to have per family?

= If I could choose I would say one or two. Now I know there is a way of choosing but I didn't know that before, so what good does it do anymore? Look at us, how old we look at just 40 years. That is because we have to work so hard for all these children. And there isn't enough food for all of us. If I had known in 1960 what I know now, I wouldn't have had all those children. And my husband would agree, I know.

– Do you ever mention that to your husband?

= Yes, I've said, "Listen, if only we had known before, we could have done something but now—it is too late!" What can we do?

– Do you think that most husbands in this village would permit their wives to control the number of pregnancies?

= Heavens, no. Few would even think of it. They say terrible things about women who want it. Some say, "The only reason you want birth control is so you can come and go, and go with other men." They think we will just go and do it with another man . . . like that . . . for no good reason.

Maria-Louisa interrupted, brusquely, saying:

= Once the radio said, "Father of families, if you want to give your children a good upbringing—then take care of them well and remember that small families live better." Well, my own brother just laughed and said, "What do you mean? Did God order that you have children? Do you think that men should take control then and order about?" You see, some people are very ignorant.

This conversation seemed to catch the fancy of the two sisters. Sophia couldn't keep from interrupting:

= The priest even agrees with the radio. But the men don't listen. The church is in favor of family planning. Once the priest said, "Look, you shouldn't have children just to have children. You should be able to take care of them, educate them, and give them all they need."

— Did the priest say this inside the church, at Mass?
= Yes, inside. He told us, "You have to know how you
want to live your life. When you have children, you have to
be able to dress them, give them food, and let them make
something of their life." Lots of people listen but most don't
understand what he is saying.
— You both have daughters; do you talk with them about
family planning?
= I have one daughter who is married but I didn't teach
her. She has two children and she learned about it herself.
The others, yes, I will teach them. I am going to tell them so
they will have a choice of what to do, how many children to
have.

Maria-Louisa joined in:

= You have to tell your daughters these days. You have to
educate them so that they know. Three children is the most
they should have. Even four is all right but no more than
four, for sure. Times have changed. We can't have ten
children anymore.

"Do you talk about family planning with other women?" I
asked the sisters.

= Yes, when I go to the river, all the women talk about it.
= I have a well, so I don't go to the river, but I do know
women who ask me about it. We talk often about such
things.
— And how did you first hear about family planning?
= I went to the health center in Oaxaca and I heard about it
there. But they told me that I would have to bring my
husband with me if I wanted to get any services. They
wanted to know if he was in agreement with such things.
That was over two years ago. My husband said he wasn't
going to take time off from the fields to go with me. That is
why I have this other child. Now I have the shots. Every
three months I go to get another shot.
— Do you have any discomfort from them?
= No. I am fine.
— What about you, Maria-Louisa?

= I got the same thing but I had lots of bleeding. Now I don't have anything. I don't want to go back there.

− I just want to ask you both two more questions. You mentioned the radio a while back. Do each of you have a radio?

Maria-Louisa said:

= I do. My sister listens with me sometimes. I like to listen to the program where people come to sing and try to get famous. The programs where they tell stories about life, I really don't understand them. I don't listen to them because I can't understand what is going on.

− But are there any programs for women, about child care or health and nutrition?

= No, I never heard of any.

− And now, the last question. I want to hear what you think about the education of boys and girls. Should they both have the same education?

Sophia turned to look at me suddenly, stating with conviction:

= I think girls should have more schooling.

The reply caught me off guard for a moment.

− Why girls?

= Because it isn't the men who educate children. It is the women who are in charge of them, who are with them all day. If the woman is ignorant how can she teach them? And, you know, the children are the future.

DOLORES HIDALGO

A drive north over the mountains from the state capital of Guanajuato brought us to Dolores Hidalgo, a town of 18,000 inhabitants. It was here, on September 16, 1810, that a liberal priest, Miguel Hidalgo y Costilla, launched the insurrection that was to result in the independence of Mexico. Dolores Hidalgo is today just another agricultural town, void of excitement or signs of progress. It calls to mind cowboy films: dust, horses, men in sombreros leaning against walls taking refuge from the sun.

The health center is housed in an old building of Spanish-Mauresque style. The large interior courtyard has a fountain in its middle; the sick wards and examining rooms are entered via the courtyard.

We talked for a while with the young doctor who is in charge of this clinic. I asked what he thought were the major cultural or attitudinal barriers to family planning efforts in this area. He replied:

= There are several. But first is the transportation problem. This health center covers a very large area; just getting to the clinic can present a problem. But let's say that a woman does get here. Then another factor becomes very important: the doctor's attitude. We have few women doctors in Mexico and rural women object to the idea that a male doctor might examine them. This is an extremely difficult cultural problem for the family planning effort. You see, in the rural areas, women are attended by midwives. That has been the custom forever and ever. She is not willing to accept that a man take care of her. He will see her body; he will even see *inside* her. This, to them, is terribly frightening.

Here in this clinic we are very lucky; we have a woman doctor. When I find that a woman would like to practice family planning, I ask her if she would prefer that the woman doctor treat her. She inevitably says, "Yes." When a woman says she doesn't want to practice family planning, I tell her that there is a possibility that a woman will treat her. Right then and there, she often changes her mind, and accepts.

− What are the other barriers?

= The religious question is a very important one, of course. In the small communities, especially, religious traditions are very strong. Other than the rhythm method, the church prohibits family planning in most areas, and if the priest is against it, progress is difficult.

Just one week ago, a woman came and told me that she wanted to remove her IUD. She said that she wanted to take Holy Communion, and the priest told her that if she had the IUD he wouldn't give it to her.

Then, too, you have still another barrier, perhaps the most important one of all: *machismo*, the attitude of the husband. Very often, husbands don't care much for their families; they don't give anything to their wives for the livelihood of the family. Yet when a wife wants to do something on her own, such as trying to limit the number of mouths to feed in the family, the husband will become angry and even beat her. He thinks it is unacceptable that she is making a decision of her own. She is challenging his authority, his power over her—and thus the very nature of his virility. The man thinks that the woman is stepping out of her sex role by making a decision on her own. She will be on the same level as him if she says whether or not she wants to have a baby. He is threatened by that freedom to decide.

Other barriers? There are the structural and service deficiencies also. But before we try to do too much about family planning problems, we should have more programs in nutrition and general health for the population.
– What are the major health problems in this area?
= Malnutrition and infectious diseases. Both derive from poverty.
– Do you have any idea what percentage of children have nutritional deficiencies?
= About 95 percent of the population.
– And what about anemia in women?
= This is something I will never understand. These women are so anemic that I wonder how they walk around—let alone how they continue to bear all these children.

The doctor accompanied us to his office where he had gathered a group of women and children to talk with us. He explained the nature of our visit to his patients and asked for their cooperation. He said, "You will be talking only among yourselves, so I'm no longer wanted here." Laughter followed his departure and soon we were participating in a lively group discussion.

Lupe was the first woman to talk with us alone. She was dressed in an orange dress and accompanied by a small girl. She told us that she had been "stolen"[2] from her parents' home, by

---

[2]The local version of elopement.

her boyfriend, in 1969. They married two years later and she now has three children.

    — How old is this child?
    = Three-and-a-half years.
    — Tell me about the changes you have observed since your mother's or grandmother's time?
    = There have been many since my grandmother's time. The only thing she knew how to do was to pray and she didn't even know to whom she was praying. But now, I can think about things and about why I am praying. I know how to read and write. I know much more than my grandmother.
    But still, I think life is just about the same. Now it is the position of men that is worse because the man has to leave the country to find work and earn money for his family. The women have only to wait and try to nourish the husband and children with the money he can earn. It is the same as in my grandmother's time. We still don't have much to eat because the wages are so very, very low.
    — What work does your husband do?
    = He is a farm laborer. Right now he works here in Mexico; he will until the harvest comes. But when the harvest is over he will have no work. He will travel to the United States and work there until he is caught by the authorities. This is the worst thing for women here; their men don't have stable work. They work for a while and then there is nothing for the family again. My husband is very good because the little he earns goes to his family. He doesn't drink or smoke.
    — Are you planning your family now?
    = Yes, with pills.
    — Do you have any side effects from them?
    = I had some pains in my stomach and went to the doctor. He told me it was not because of the pills.
    — Does your husband agree about the use of contraceptives?
    = Yes.
    — And what about the priest here, what does he say?
    = It is forbidden, he says it is forbidden.
    — Are you a Catholic?
    = Yes, but I haven't gone to see the priest about this. I go to

Mass but I don't go to confession. If I did, I would have to confess that I am taking the pill.
— What would the priest say?
= He would tell me to leave the church. He would not give me Holy Communion.

The woman began to show signs of uneasiness as we talked about the church and the role of the priest. I thought best to change the subject of our conversation by asking:

— What do you want most for your children in their later lives?
= I want them to get an education so they won't be in this misery like us.
— And do you think that boys and girls should be educated equally?
= My children are girls so it is not my problem, but I think mothers care more about the education of boys because it is the boys who will need more education in the future.
— One last question: how much does your husband earn when he works here in Mexico?
= Five *pesos* a day (20 cents U.S.). But when he goes to the United States he earns much, much more. But it depends on how much time it takes for the immigration officials to catch him and send him back to Mexico. Sometimes that happens right away. The most he was ever able to stay was two months.

The second woman was much older. Her face was sunbeaten and wrinkled, her shoulders stooped. Her clothes told of her poverty; her features revealed her Indian ancestry. She wore a faded green shawl over her head and her eyes were lowered as if she were sad or not too sure of her own feelings.
She told us she was 55 years old and that her husband had died several years ago. She is illiterate.

— How many children do you have?
= I had 15. Only 7 remain; all the others are dead.
— Did they die as children?
= Yes, when they were very small.
— Do you know the cause of their deaths?

= Maybe it was because of the hunger. We were very, very poor. My husband earned only 3 pesos a week. Our life was very bad. I didn't have any shoes, nor clothes. Every night I would wash my clothes and put them on again in the morning. We didn't have anything.

– What kind of work did your husband do?

= He was a farm laborer but my mother-in-law took all the money he earned; she was the one who gave us some food. She was the administrator of the money. She just gave us beans to eat all the time. I was always very weak because of so little food. I think that is why the babies died.

Some died while I was nursing them, others at about one year of age.

– Was your husband a good man?

= At the end he was better but at first he wasn't nice with me. He beat me and screamed at me all the time. I would run and hide when I saw him coming for I knew he would beat me. He would drink with his mother and then beat me. He was like that for about 15 years and then, somehow, he changed. We spent 16 lovely years together until he died.

– How do you live now that he is dead?

= I have been working, doing some laundry, when there is some to do. I sent the children to be shepherds for a man who has lots of animals. He used to give the children some food to eat. I have one son who goes to the United States very often and he sends me money when he has it. Another son is 15 years old; he works but not every day because there is not much work here. I don't have much money, just what the two sons can find to give me.

– Have you seen much change in the lives of women since you were a young girl?

= Before, women were very stupid; they didn't realize what life was because they didn't have any education or anything. Now women are beginning to go to work or to go to school and they are beginning to know other things. They can have more control over their lives now.

– What do you think women here need most in order to improve their lives?

= The biggest problems of this town are drunkenness and poverty. The men get drunk and spend all the money they have. When I think of it I become sad because I remember the bad times I had with a drunken husband and such terrible poverty.

— Does the priest try to tell the men how to behave?

= There's preaching, to be sure, but nobody understands it. The men don't pay any attention. The only people who go to Mass are women. In this whole town there are only five men who go to church. Men couldn't care less about what the priest says, since they don't go to church anyway.

— Did any of your children go to school?

= Two of the boys went and so did one girl for a time. They attended primary school. They wanted to study more but we couldn't afford it.

The conversation was disturbing the woman deeply. She looked up at the interpreter and said, "I am ashamed to be telling such sad stories, but it is the truth. My life has not been good."

I took her hand in mine and told her that her life was not very different from those of many women I had met in these travels, that she should not be ashamed to speak from the heart as she wanted. Then I asked,

— If you had had a good husband and a better life, would you have wanted to have as many children as you did?

= Yes, because it is God's will. I know there are ways to stop having children now, but the priest does not permit it. He says it is evil. I think he is wrong to say that.

The reason I am here today is to see my daughter. She is here in the hospital. She has just had a Cesarean birth. It was her ninth child but it was born dead. The doctor is asking for 4,000 pesos as payment, and her husband doesn't know how he is going to pay. He is a laborer and they have seven children. There are so many to feed. He earns only 25 pesos a day. How is he going to find the money to pay?

— How long has your daughter been in the hospital?

= Just one day but she has to be here eight days more. The doctor told her to buy the medicine she needs because they don't have it here. But we don't have the money to buy it, and I am afraid she will get sick and die. I am frightened that they won't let her out of the hospital if we can't pay the doctor.

As the woman told us this story, tears began to fall. She sighed quietly. She was terrorized by the idea that her daughter might lose her health or that she be kept there in the hospital because she couldn't pay.

= Every time we come here we have to pay. That is why we don't come often. My daughter is 36 years old and she has all these children. Seven of them are living. Last year she was having a miscarriage and we came to get the nurse from the hospital but, by the time she arrived, the baby was dead. This time, after the Cesarean, the doctor tied her tubes.

I agree with that. How can she go on like this, without any money to pay and to feed the children? Her husband is happy to know about it, because they are very poor and he doesn't like to see his wife suffer like this. My daughter is happy, also.

The old woman permitted me to go with her to visit her daughter. When I left the two women together, I sought out the doctor who, only a few hours before, had told us that this hospital was free for those who had no means to pay for its services. I explained the situation, saying that at the rate of 25 pesos per day, it would take the father six months to earn the sum he was asked to pay for his wife's operation. What were his wife and children to eat in the meantime?

My words resulted in obvious consternation, a flurry of activity, and a conversation between the doctor and the husband. What happened thereafter I do not know.

VILLAGRANDE

Villagrande is a *bourg* of 28,000 inhabitants who labor in the fields of the rich El Bahio region. Wheat, barley, maize, and alfalfa are grown here as are the fruits sold to the large canneries whose smoke pollutes the skies above the town. Few of the people are landowners; most of them work on the large estates for 5 to 25 pesos per day. I was told that Villagrande has a serious malnutrition problem. I also learned that most of the produce of this region is reserved for export.

Upon arrival at the health clinic in the early morning, we

found rows of women waiting for the medical consultations to begin. They wore shawls around their shoulders or over their heads. Each was accompanied by a number of small children.

The first woman to speak with us openly told me about hiding her use of contraceptives from her husband.

She was small and slim in pants and a T-shirt. Her hair was pulled back neatly in a tiny chignon. With her was a nicely dressed 3-year old daughter and a smaller child barely old enough to stand. The mother told us she was 19 years old, that she had gone to school for awhile and had learned to read and write a little. "But," she added, "the teacher didn't come to school very often, so we didn't learn very much." She had really taught herself to read. Her father had been very poor. She had started working at the age of ten in order to help the family, which had six children in all. She smiled as she talked, then added:

= I have been married for four years; I have just these two children you see here. The first is three, the other almost one year.

I was stunned by the youthful appearance of this woman, but saddened by what I perceived as a tinge of resignation in her voice. I asked:

− When we talked in the group with other women earlier, they mentioned that one of the changes they have witnessed in the last few generations is access to education. What do you think are the other changes?
= The first thing that makes the times different, I think, is the control women have over the number of children in a family. A family can be planned now; it can live a better life. Women have more facilities for everything because of this. I began to take contraceptives when this last child was eight months old. I take the pill.
− Do you want more children later?
= My husband wants a boy because these are both girls. He doesn't know that I am taking the pill. He wants a boy and says that when I have one, then I can use contraceptives. I want to wait at least two years so that this little girl is older. Then I will try for the boy.

– Do you talk about this openly with your husband?
= No, almost never. In fact, my husband has a sister who is using a contraceptive method. She asked me if I was interested in using one and I said, "No," because I didn't want her to tell my husband. He might find out that I already use them. I just want to wait a few years and rest. When I wanted the pills I came here to the health center. They didn't have any so I went to see an aunt. She gave me some.
– But how do you hide the pills? Where do you keep them so they won't be discovered?
= I keep them in the kitchen. When I'm cooking dinner, I take a pill and he doesn't notice. Either that or I take one while he is sleeping. But you know, all this is very dangerous, because my husband went to school; he is smart, and he knows about such things.

And once he did find them. I was terribly frightened. I had hidden them in a closet, under some clothes. He found them and asked, "What are these pills?" I just said that my baby daughter had found them and brought them into the house. I told him I took them away from her because she was going to eat them.

My husband told me, "You know, these pills are very dangerous because they are for not having children. If I find out that you are taking them, you will see what I will do to you!"
– Did he threaten you?
= Yes, he threatened to hit me. He is very suspicious. It seems strange to him that this girl here is already one year old and I am not pregnant again. He keeps asking me why I'm not pregnant, telling me to go to the doctor and see about it. He says, "Even if you don't want any more children, I want at least one boy. After that, you can do what you want."
– Do you think that family planning is very important to the women you know? Do you know many women who take contraceptives?
= For me it is very important because my husband does not earn big wages. For the moment we just can't afford more than two children.

— What do you want most for your children in later life?

= You know, I was very poor. We were six children and my father didn't earn much money. That is why I want just two or three children because I don't want my children to grow up with no education like me.

I feel very ashamed and bad about not having any education. I want my children to go to school and learn many, many things. I don't want them to live by the rumors of the street; I want them to learn for themselves. I want them to be independent of others and proud of themselves.

As I opened the door to the hallway to ask the next woman to enter, the noise of the waiting women and children came to us again. As in most places in the world, here the waiting period at a health clinic is a time to exchange news and gossip with women from different neighborhoods. It was a busy, happy noise, despite the whining and cries of the small, impatient, bored children.

Isabella is 30 years old. She appeared tired that morning as she held a small child on her lap and talked with us. She said that she had lived alone with her father because her mother had abandoned her to run off with another man. She had gone to school for just three years and then, because of the death of her father, she had lived until her marriage with an aunt and uncle.

She has five children. The eldest is ten, the youngest one year and eight months. She hurried to explain, "I married when I was 16, but I didn't get pregnant until I was almost 20."

— Do you want more children, Isabella?

= No, I don't want any more because I am tired and sick. I have had pains in the stomach for quite some time now. The examinations don't show anything wrong but it frightens me. Since I began to have those pains I came here and asked for the pill. I am taking them now.

— Did your husband also want you to use a contraceptive method?

= He didn't want it at first. He said that the whole town would laugh at him if he didn't have any more children. They would say that his virility is over, gone.

But I was so frightened by these pains that I went to the

priest. I thought if the priest said it was all right, maybe my husband would accept it, too. Also, I knew that if I had more children, I would surely die.

− Tell me what happened.

= First I asked my husband's permission and he said no. But then I thought about asking the priest. I got a certificate from the doctor saying that I was ill. I took the certificate to the priest and told him that I was feeling very, very weak and poorly.

The priest said, "Yes, go to the center and ask for something for not having children."

Then I went to my husband and told him that I had gone to the priest and that he had said it was all right. I told him, "You know, five is enough. I don't want to give you any more children."

− Does the priest ever mention family responsibility or family planning in church?

= Family responsibility, yes. He tells about it every Sunday. He is always telling the people not to have many children and to be responsible for them, to give them a good education, to give them careers, and to raise them in a good way. But he doesn't mention family planning. Never. It was only because I proved that I was sick that he agreed to let me do it.

− Do you know any other women who plan their families?

= No. I don't think many women do because they think that they might go to hell if they do. And then they are afraid of the pills. They say they are harmful. But I don't care anymore. I have so much pain that I don't care about that. I want to take the pill anyway.

− And what about the husbands? Do they want to have as many children as come, despite what the priest says?

= There are very few men who follow the counsel of the priest. Most men drink a lot and go with women. They have many vices. They are not responsible for their families at all because they like to drink too much and to have other women. And they beat their wives.

My husband used to drink a lot also. But he joined Alcoholics Anonymous and he is a better man now, to his family and to me.

IN THE SUBURBS

Built upon the dried bed of a salt lake on the outskirts of Mexico City stands one of its many "transition towns," a stopping place for the thousands of people who come to the city each week in search of work and of respite from the poor life of landless peasantry. What they find, usually, is more poverty, greater disdain for their kind, and an unsanitary existence. Ciudad Netzahualcoyotl is a shanty town where few speak the dialect of the neighbor next door and where few social relationships can be established.

There is no plumbing here. Pot-bellied children play amidst trash blown about with the dust of the treeless landscape and chew on dirty sugar cane stalks. Sick dogs scavenge for food among the debris. Young men lean against the shacks, waiting for those who work in the city beyond to return and tell them what is happening in the other world.

We drove through Netzahualcoyotl's endless unpaved streets on our way to another suburb of the city; the interpreter had wanted me to see the kind of place through which 1,000 migrants who come to Mexico City each day pass before they are integrated into the life of the metropolis—sometimes two or three generations later.

The women in the department store in a lower-middle-class suburb where we were headed are only a generation or two removed from such "transition cities". The wives or daughters of skilled laborers, they attend a self-improvement class at the store in an attempt to improve their education and their social graces.

Luisa was dressed in a neat cotton suit. Her hair was short and her manner modern, self-assured. She smiled as we began our conversation, saying that she was 30 years old, married, and the mother of two children, three years and one year old.

— What do you think have been the changes in women's lives in the last two generations, Luisa?
= Freedom, I think, is the most important change. The older generation had to stay within the home. We, today, are free to move about, to work, or not work. It is very different for modern women. Even the children nowadays

are allowed to participate in discussions at home. Before, it was only the grandparents who spoke; everyone else had to remain silent. You see, I had a very strict upbringing and I know things have changed greatly.

– How did you meet your husband?

= Through another friend. I met him 12 years ago. I wasn't looking for anything special, just a good relationship. I love him and he loves me. We are happy together.

Our son and daughter are fine but he thinks the children are my responsibility. Just me, alone. He wants me to take care of their education but he keeps telling me to study more because I need to know more so I can be a better mother. I try to learn many things but it is difficult because I don't know any people who can guide me. I am too much alone. I want to learn how to be a good mother but I don't know what it is I should learn.

My mother always said, "You can't do anything." She was an ignorant woman; she didn't even know how to read or write. So I forgive her for the way she treated me. But my father was a different case. He told me I had to learn, but he never taught me how. I am angry with him because he was intelligent but he never knew how to teach me. I want to learn how to be intelligent, to know things, and how to teach.

When my husband tells me to study, he says it is for my son—so my son will have an intelligent mother, but I think a daughter is just as important as a son. Right now my daughter is always afraid of doing things. She is very nice but not very aggressive. She is too feminine. I want her to be herself, and play like the boys if she wants to.

– What do you want most for your children later?

= I don't care if they want to be this or that. They can study what they want. I just want them to feel well within themselves. They should have a good basic education, a firm moral basis to go on in life because I believe that in the end we are always alone. They should learn how to be independent.

– Do you want more children?

= Right now, two is enough. I have an IUD because I keep thinking that perhaps one day we will not have enough money to pay for more than two children. I wanted to have my tubes tied but the doctors said that I was too young. I told them, "It is not *you* who have the children. If I have another child I will bring it to you to raise and feed."

Here in Mexico, believe me, it is very difficult. Most doctors won't help you, even with money. You are afraid to go to the free clinics because they make you wait, or say come back in another week, and then they don't even examine you properly. I decided that I would rather pay than have it done by people who don't take their work seriously. You know, if they are not careful, you can get cancer or something like that.

– How much did you pay for your IUD?

= Three thousand pesos ($150 U.S.). But I am glad I did it because my husband doesn't want me to have the operation. Yet at the same time he doesn't bother to do anything to prevent us from having more children. He is a Catholic and he doesn't like to talk about such things. He says it is a crime to have an abortion. But to me it is more of a crime to have a child and not be able to feed it properly and give it a good life.

If I am going to have more children, who is going to feed them? When my children are crying, is it God who comes to comfort them? You know, the priests say it is a sin not to have the children that come . . . and that influences a lot of people.

– Do you have many women friends who use contraceptives?

= That depends on the social classes. The wives of my husband's friends are afraid of them. They think it is good to have many children because it pleases their husbands. When we talk about it the women get angry with me.

The husband will say, "Yes," or "No," or "It is *her* problem." The wife says, "My mother thinks I should have more," or "I don't want to have problems with my husband." But, in fact, they just continue on and have more children. I don't think they talk to each other very much.

But the women of the lower classes have a different method, the one they have been using for generations. They practice abortion to limit the number of children in the family. They don't even question if it is good or bad for their health or for religion. They just do it. They do it because it is the only method they know for family planning. I know a woman, a maid who works in our building, who has five children. She told me she had already had four abortions. Her husband never knew. And that is the key to the whole question. He doesn't know and she would never tell him. This way they can plan their families without the husband's permission.

There she is, 40 years old, five children and four abortions. And she aborted only because she didn't have the money for more children. She lives in the caves of Aero este Paderna. Most of the people there are migrants from the country. They live in the caves because they are so very poor. She told me about a midwife who delivers babies and performs all the functions of a doctor. The midwife told Alma to take a fork and introduce it inside the vagina. She did. She bled a lot so she had to go to the hospital and stay there.

The doctor took care of her but he didn't tell her anything about family planning or anything else. She was so frightened she didn't dare ask him. So another pregnancy came and the same thing happened. She went to the midwife a second time. But this time, I think, it wasn't a fork, but a knife or something that cut the vagina. Well, this went on until the last time when she went to the hospital in an emergency and the doctor recognized her. He said, "What is wrong? What happened to you?"

She told him she didn't want to have another child so he asked if she wanted to have her tubes tied. So, finally, after all this hell, she found a way to be helped. And this is the way it is for many women.

VIII WOMEN, MEN,
THE FAMILY

*"Why do we always talk of women as
'mother' and never of men as 'father'?"*
Helvi Sipila,[1] Cairo, 1972

The conversations in this report cannot, in any way, be considered a "scientific" sampling of the views of rural women the world over. They do, however, reflect the opinions of many, as the repetition in the individual testimonies attests. The very repetitiveness of the answers to my questions, despite vast cultural differences among the women speaking in six nations, adds, I think, a new dimension to our understanding of rural women's lives and the commonality of their concerns. Over and over, in Africa, in Asia, and in the New World, they spoke of the absence of choice in their lives, of the lack of personal autonomy. They would like to have more control over their destinies, to be able to choose their mates and the size of their families, to participate in society, and to contribute to it.

The barriers to those goals are many. In some places, new basic laws and social regulations are needed. In others, women's legal rights exist but are not understood as well as they might be or enforced as they should be. And everywhere literacy, skill-training, self-confidence, and personal autonomy are required to overcome the myths, taboos, traditions, and male supremacy that stifle women's wish to participate.

Most disabling of all, and influencing everything else, is the

---

[1] Assistant Secretary-General for Centre for Social Development and Humanitarian Affairs.

fear of male dominance: wife-beating, polygamy, restricted mobility, and lack of legal protection continue to hold women in resigned apathy.

And it starts early. A father's approval or disapproval of a daughter's attendance at school can give her an opportunity to learn or—keep her in ignorance forever. Young girls yearn for a husband "who will talk" with them, for they know so well that communication between husband and wife is often rare. Only those women who had been able to choose their husbands had, sometimes, a successful dialogue within their marriages.

Women, subject to the whims of their men—through divorce, polygamy, inheritance inequities, abandonment and, it should be added, alcoholism—dare not move out of their restricted roles. The price women pay, everywhere in the developing world, remains too great. The family—women, men and children—and the development process itself suffers as a result.

The strong relationship between the status of women, population programs and overall development policy has been recognized for some time. But at present it unfortunately appears that women have, in most cases, been victimized (once again) by development policies. The old patriarchal division of labor has been cast out in many post-colonial economies. In some cases, men have been attracted into the service of multinational interests, cash-cropping, or the political-economic programs of the nations' leadership. Women have been left behind to rear children and take on a larger share of the menial—traditional—tasks. They take on the additional burdens "progress" has given them, they continue to strive for the well-being of their families, but they receive few rewards. Women stressed these phenomena when they told me of the increasing economic differences between them and their husbands, and of the decline of male responsibility toward the family. They say development policies are favoring men and, thus, sadly, widening the economic and communications gap between men and women. Throughout their conversations, one finds a plea that men and women "work together", "plan together" for the benefit of the family and the nation.

If we can consider the opinions of the women I interviewed as representative of those of the rural developing world—and I believe they are—we must quickly reexamine our population and development policies. Social change demands a transformation of laws, customs, thought-patterns and education. It starts in the home; it depends on women as much as men. A non-person cannot raise responsible adults of the future. The advancement of women directly affects the well-being of their societies.

As women in developing nations face growing economic pressures and take on added burdens of labor due to the transformation of traditional economies and sex roles, the many children they traditionally bear have become—in this time of change—an extra economic burden. Children must be fed, cared for and clothed. If they go to school, even when schooling is free, they must have shoes, pencils and notebooks. More and more, rural families tend to consider that education and training are the means via which to obtain salaried work; they want their children to attend school rather than toil in the fields. Due to the changing economy and to changing attitudes toward education the children who were once prized as units of production within the family, are now costing the family precious cash. Women, because they often assure the survival needs of the family, are all too aware of this. Irrespective of religious or ethnic background, most of the women I interviewed believe that if they are to extricate themselves from the cycle of poverty, their children must have "more chances than I did" or "become educated". To provide those chances or education, women know they must have smaller families than before—and they know that now, thanks to the new availability of health services, in most areas, infant mortality has declined and they no longer need to have 15 children to assure that four or five reach adulthood.

Like all the mothers of the world, most of the village women I met echoed, "It is a joy to have children . . . but only if they are healthy, educated, and can have some cause for hope." The more women I met, the more I heard their wish for "quality of children" as distinct from the "quantity of children". They share a common understanding that their own "old age security" lies in the education or training of their children and *not* in their numbers.

Why then, do so many rural couples even now continue to have so many children? Because the majority of women with whom I spoke told me they have little choice in the matter of family planning.

BARRIERS TO FAMILY PLANNING

Religion did not often surface as an important barrier to a woman's acceptance of contraceptive methods. When a woman's personal religious beliefs prohibited the use of a contraceptive, some said they were willing to "sin" because they can no longer cope with the growing number of mouths to feed. Women did sometimes cite a husband's religious convictions, however, as the reason *he* had forbidden her to seek family planning services.

Understanding male attitudes relevant to family needs and responsibility is crucial to the design and operation of successful family planning efforts. Without the consent of their husbands, women are not, and will not be for some time, free to use a contraceptive.

Women say they have to have their husband's permission to go to the health clinic—they fear the husband's wrath if they do not become pregnant each year—or they know the husband can divorce them or take another wife if he is not continually pleased. Husbands, they claim, want, for a variety of reasons, to keep the wives burdened with pregnancies. Cowed by custom and fear, too few women dare question male authority.

For this reason, it is my belief that women are not those who need to be convinced of the benefits of family planning. Their menfolk—husbands or national, village and religious leaders—need the convincing. I believe male dominance of women's lives is the largest single barrier to effective population efforts. Family planning programs must attempt to sensitize men to the notion of family health and family responsibility, because the success of those efforts ultimately depends on the support and encouragement of men—either on the personal level of husband or on the national level of male policy-makers who control the decisions on sex education in schools, the support of women's organizations, or the use of the media as an effective learning tool.

Unfortunately, on all those levels, one often encounters opposition from change-resistant men.

In the preceding chapters, we have heard cries from the hearts of women themselves about their husbands' attitudes. It is possibly even more disturbing to encounter the attitudes of some policy-makers who espouse outmoded theories on the roles of women while continuing to influence the national bi-lateral and international agencies which are mandated to aid the rural family. During this survey I met male officials, sitting in air-conditioned offices, who scoffed at me for wanting to visit remote rural areas: "Why do you want to go there, to talk with ignorant people?" The implication was clear: I shouldn't bother.

Fortunately, not all officials are so insensitive. One, who has many years of experience in the field of population policy, explained, "The problem is simple. The experts arrive in a country and, being men, they spend a few days visiting the city and talking with other men. Then they go away and write reports for reading by more men." Ignoring the realities of rural life —or those of women's existence—these officials are guilty of a de-structive misinterpretation of women's needs. The programs they design reinforce the notion that contraception is a woman's problem *only*. Worse still, by preaching family planning *only to women*, they contribute to disharmony between husband and wife.

Many have spoken out against this attitudinal bias. Mallica Vajrathon, for one, has written extensively about the one-sided prejudice of family planning efforts, noting, "We should avoid producing materials that blame only women as non-stop breed-ing machines and assert that the problem of over-population occurs because women are ignorant".[2]

And Erskine Childers, of the United Nations Development Programme writes, "It is difficult to conceive of any significant, sustained effort to generate and design the kind of programs and projects that are needed if the assumption is that no prior, or at least simultaneous, effort needs to be made to start to change the basic prejudices among at least the most directly involved men".[3]

The intellectual and emotional attitudes of program design-ers, administrators, and policy-makers is part of the population problem—and of its solution.

[2]*Changing of Individual Attitudes and Values in Population and Family Planning —Human Roles Versus Traditional Sex-roles.* East-West Communi-cations Institute, December 1975.

[3]Statement to the Seminar on Women in Development, American Association for the Advancement of Science, 1975.

TOWARD MORE SENSITIVE PROGRAMS

Rafael M. Salas, Executive Director of the United Nations Fund for Population Activities, states, "The pursuit of a successful population policy and full equality for women both imply that women must be involved in formulating and carrying out that policy".[4]

There will be those who suggest that few "qualified" women can be found for population policy positions. Yet I met many well-educated and concerned women in each nation, whose experience and skills would be greatly beneficial to population programs. The justification for their involvement is simple. When dealing with such a delicate subject as that of family planning, only women have access to the intimate thoughts of other women. Only women know the reality of other women's lives. They know too well about the lack of freedom of decision and about male dominance. They know that family planning information must be simultaneously directed at men. Their involvement in the design and delivery of family planning programs is fundamental.

THE ROLE OF LEADERSHIP

The World Population Plan of Action, approved in Bucharest in 1974, stated, "All couples and individuals have the basic human right to decide freely and responsibly the number and spacing of their children and to have the information, education, and means to do so."[5]

This is a clear call to the leaders of nations to give serious attention to the family planning needs of their peoples. Yet those who have done so are the exceptions. The woman who said "leaders are not guiding us; they really don't care about us" voiced a feeling expressed by many other women with whom I spoke.

Too often, at the highest level, there is a lack of commitment to involve women in the development process as a whole, to support women's efforts to help themselves and each other, and to unequivocally supporting national family planning ef-

[4]*The Freedom to Choose.* Address to the International Women's Conference, Mexico City, July 1975.

[5]World Population Plan of Action, Chapter II, para 14 (f).

forts, both morally and structurally. Again, we come face to face with an attitudinal problem—the paying of little more than "lip service" to women's integration in the development process.

Mme. Jehan Sadat of Egypt gave me an example of the disinterest she encounters. She told me that whenever she is in the presence of a Minister of State, she raises the family planning issue, saying, "Please don't forget this problem because whatever you do, it is nothing compared to what you will have to do because we are adding 1 million (people) every year (to our population)." The Egyptian President's wife went on to say that some of those ministers are not always responsive "to the degree I feel necessary".

Whether or not the absence of effective leadership in family planning is based on political reasons, or lack of vision, the problem remains the same. Alone, women are nearly powerless to advance, participate, and accept available services. They must be supported and encouraged by the men who influence, or control, their lives. Without this support they can only work the land, strive to raise their children in dignity, and, ultimately, be blamed for their "ignorance", i.e., lack of personal autonomy.

SOME POSSIBLE RESOURCES

In conversations with rural women and family planning personnel, several resources were named as being already available but not effectively used. These include:

Women's organizations. This powerful force for change remains largely ignored by family planning program designers. In cultures where most information received by women comes from other women, the role of women's organizations is crucial. Skill development, literacy training, leadership training, family planning, education in all forms can be delivered through existing women's organization networks. In fact, for most male-dominated rural areas, it is probably the most practical means of reaching women.

Women's organizations, however, are everywhere distinguished by their lack of funds. It is true that most are, at least in the urban centers, composed of female members of a country's elite. Being well-off, however, does not necessarily mean that these women, although they may be able to volunteer their services, can afford the tools to work with people in rural areas. They need financial support for transportation, teaching aids, and expenses. Also moral support from leadership is also extremely important. In countries where women have just begun to participate in community life, a husband's—or neighbor's—mockery can stifle the desire to serve. Where a woman's participation is associated with prestige and recognized by the country's leaders, resistance is minimized.

"Elite women, especially those in high status positions", Adrienne Germain[6] has pointed out, "may help create new attitudes toward women and effect change." In their capacity of change agent, women's organization members serve as role models for other women. Many rural women told me of their wish to serve others "just as the women (of a named organization) served us." In cases where women have themselves, at the local level, taken the initiative to start self-help projects or cooperatives, government agencies should support their efforts through counsel, funds, and encouragement.

The Media. This source of influence on the lives of millions can be criticized almost everywhere for its lack of practical teaching programs even though in most developing countries, radio, and television are controlled by the government and a ministry of information or culture decides program content. Among the women I spoke with, few said that they received helpful information from the media whether on family planning or education in any form. Many said there should be more "women's programs" or those which deal with "family life." Others suggested programs on cooking (nutrition), health and agriculture. A second preference was for "news broadcasts". Almost everyone complained that there were not enough of these programs or that they were broadcast at times when women were elsewhere, "digging in the fields", or "at market".

A commitment from national leaders to provide more information of practical educational value to rural families—both men and women—through the media would undoubtedly benefit development/family planning programs.

Sex education. At the earliest age possible, sex education should be made available—and given top priority as part of

[6]*Status and Roles of Women as Factors in Fertility Behavior: A Policy Analysis.* Population Council, July 1975.

family planning efforts. In some cultures modesty prevents women from discussing intimate relations even with their daughters; in Kenya, for example, I was told that many young school girls become pregnant without knowing the reason why.

The 10-year-olds of today will be of marriageable age within the next four to five years; sex education, coupled with family responsibility/family planning courses, should be an integral part of their early learning process. As many women stressed, "It is too late for me, but I hope my children will have smaller families". And the sons must be taught about family planning, just as much as the daughters.

This "men also" concern is crucial. One woman I interviewed boldly asked: "Why do women have to use all the contraceptives? Why don't men start too? Be sure and go back and tell the UN that men should use contraceptives also; they should invent a pill for men." She thought men ought to take their responsibility toward the family, saying, "Remember we are supposed to be partners".

It is this sense of responsibility, too often failed, of men for women, for families, that echoes most strongly throughout the conversations with the women I met. Without exception, those interviewed were seeking a better existence for their families and a better relationship with their menfolk. They do not think of themselves as separate beings, divorced from the male world. They want to be part of the change taking place around them, they want to prepare their children for the world of the future, they want to "work together with men" and build a life of service and harmony. The high value placed on the family structure is the very essence of their lives.

As we ponder the complexities of development of population policy we must go beyond the considerations of GNP, statistics and charts. We must ask: are we taking into consideration the values, needs and hopes of the rural family? Are we doing our best to understand the aspirations of all members of the family? Are we sufficiently aware of the enormous potential offered by the full participation of women in the development effort?

The situation of each woman interviewed here is unique yet each woman sends the very same message: women must be involved in development programs; the attitudes of men must be considered in population strategies; rural peoples must be consulted in both development and family planning efforts.

In recent years we have come to realize that the global problems of our times need cooperative solutions. We have seen that we must guard against the destruction of the values and dignity of citizens of the developing world. Collaborative efforts in the design and delivery of population development programs are indispensable. The women I met pointed out that this is true at their level. Their words suggest that it is true at the international policy level as well.